S0-ACC-411

THE PHANTOMS OF DIXIE

HANS HOLZER

THE PHANTOMS OF DIXIE

THE BOBBS-MERRILL COMPANY, INC.
Indianapolis and New York

The Bobbs-Merrill Company, Inc.
Indianapolis • New York

Library of Congress catalogue card number 71-188653
Designed by A. Christopher Simon
Illustrated by Catherine Buxhoeveden

Manufactured in the United States of America

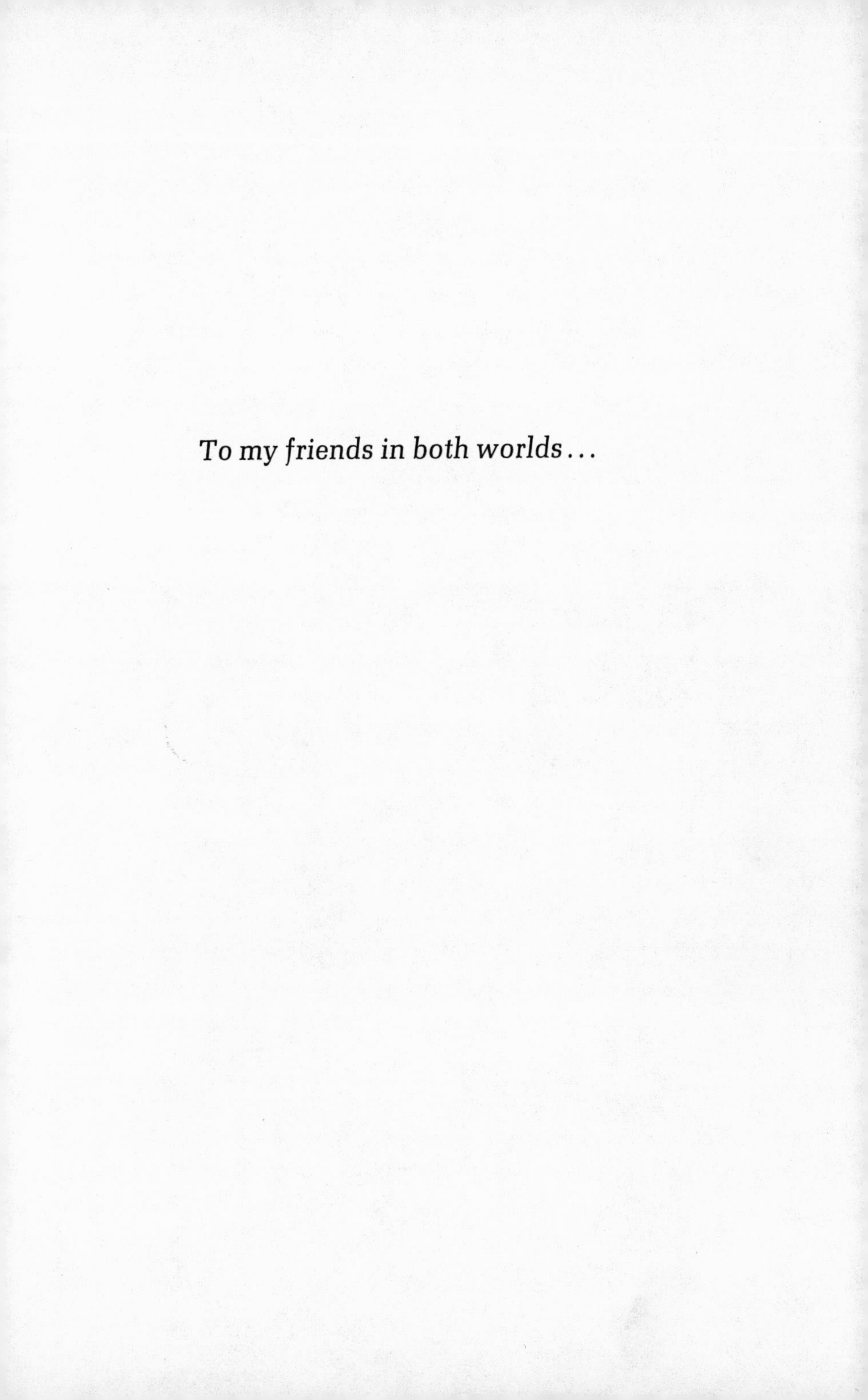

To my friends in both worlds . . .

CONTENTS

FOREWORD ix

ALABAMA 3
ARKANSAS 17
FLORIDA 23
GEORGIA 31
LOUISIANA 51
MARYLAND 57
NORTH CAROLINA 69
OKLAHOMA 93
SOUTH CAROLINA 99
TEXAS 105
THE DEVIL IN TEXAS 125
VIRGINIA 199

FOREWORD

Dixie is not a place; it's a state of mind. To some, it is a healthy state of mind because it divides the United States into two distinct political and cultural zones. To others the term is a very sentimental one because it signifies a romantic world nonexistent in many parts of the country yet still preserved in the conservative older sections of our South. Whatever interpretation one wishes to put on the word Dixie it is a term readily understood by everyone. There is no need to be apologetic about using it. So vast a country as the United States of America is bound to have regional differences and peculiarities. The New Englander is just as proud of his heritage and way of life as is the Californian, or any other native of the country. Dixie simply refers to the southern states. Its geographical boundaries are somewhat vague at times, because there are states not properly within the defined area of Dixie yet close to it. In this collection of cases, I have confined myself to what are generally referred to as the southern states. Oklahoma, which to many represents a western state, has been included since a large portion of that state does lie within the boundaries of the South. The term Dixie, incidentally, is derived from the Mason-Dixon Line, a somewhat arbitrary border between the northern and the southern states. This line was established at the time of the Industrial Revolution when it was becoming more and more clear that the South would develop along different lines than the industrial North. Those who lived above the Mason-Dixon Line were then considered northerners, while the territory below the line constituted the South.

Theoretically, the War between the States abolished the inequities between the people who lived north of the Mason-Dixon Line and those who lived south of it. But it is only now that the Bill of Rights is being put into full effect in this respect and that the wounds of the Civil War are gradually healing. However, from the time of the War between the States to the recent congressional moves toward racial integration there has been an unspoken boundary between the northern and southern states: a border that wasn't marked on any map but nevertheless existed as a reality. Until a few years ago to cross the Mason-Dixon Line meant, in some respects, exactly what it had meant before the War between the States.

The natural character of Southerners in the United States is, of course, similar to that of southern people anywhere else in the world. They live at a slower pace than their northern brethren; appreciate a life of comfort; hold to conservative political views rather than the more radical revolutionary ones; favor an agricultural society over an industrial one; and even their speech is slower, more melodic, perhaps even more slurred than that of their more precise, somewhat nervously motivated northern neighbors. This is not a development unique to America; it exists also in Italy, Austria, Germany, and even France, where the Southerner, or meridional, is a distinctive type. Tension exists between north and south in these lands just as it exists in this country. On the other hand, the Southerners have been responsible for much of the cultural development in all of these cases simply because Southerners have more time for leisure, more time to ruminate about their past, and are perhaps more conscious of their ties to past values and traditions. It would be foolish to assume that the pronounced difference between North and South in the United States is merely due to the question of black people and their role in the economy. That may have been the main issue just before the Civil War when the problem was chiefly an economic one and the large plantations relied very heavily on slave labor. But it is not a vital issue today, and yet the differences between North and South remain pronounced.

The slower, more tradition-bound atmosphere of the southern states tends to encourage a preoccupation with the occult. The personal attitude of many Southerners toward the unseen differs sharply from that of the Northerner. Up North there is less time for psychic phenomena. In the South one takes these things in stride, especially when the story being told is romantic and interesting. And Southerners are great storytellers. Then too there are a number of large old manor houses in the southern states which compare favorably with European castles. They were built by families of long standing and great repute, many of whom came over a long time ago from Europe, and their homes represent a continuing emotional tie with the past. There is less of this feeling in the northern states, where the great houses were built mainly by industrial barons or by the *nouveau riche*.

Another aspect of the southern attitude toward the unseen can be gleaned from the makeup of the population.

The southern states are less polyglot and in the main populated by people of Anglo-Saxon extraction. Now it is a fact that the Scottish, English, and Irish people have a greater leaning toward the psychic than have, let us say, the French or German nationals. Why this is so is difficult to determine unless, indeed, the Celtic heritage still pulsates in so many of these people. From their ancestral homes in the British Isles many of these Southerners have derived a respect for the occult which makes them more receptive to reports dealing with occurrences of seemingly illogical events. The atmosphere for ghosts, hauntings, psychic dreams and such is far more open in the South than in the urban North. It is perhaps no coincidence that the most prominent center for parapsychological studies is at the University of Virginia in Charlottesville, Virginia.

Several years ago I wrote *Yankee Ghost*. In that book I was able to convey the flavor of New Englanders and of their ghosts by reporting in their own words how these people felt when faced with the uncanny.

I can do no less for the South.

The stories in this book are arranged alphabetically by states. Most of the southern states are represented, although not in the same measure. This is not because there are proportionately fewer ghosts in, let us say, Tennessee than there are in Texas but simply that more Texas ghosts have come to my attention. Because of its size, the number of psychic occurrences reported from the area of Texas is naturally numerically larger than those from, let us say, North or South Carolina. But even within the framework of the Dixie states there are marked differences in the nature of these phantoms. The flavor differs from the Carolinas to the Gulf Coast, from southern Oklahoma to Tidelands Virginia.

THE PHANTOMS OF DIXIE

ALABAMA

Not unlike the roll call at the national conventions I will call upon the shades of various southern states to come forward with the accounts of their psychic activities. I am speaking to you not only of haunted houses and ghosts seen or heard by living people but also of people who are themselves gifted with the ability to experience communications from the other world. This is as it should be, for where would the phantoms of Dixie be if it were not for flesh and blood people to acknowledge them, to help them understand themselves at times, or at least to relate their unhappy past?

Mrs. Nancy Anglin originally contacted me when I collected material on reincarnation cases for a previous book called *Born Again*. Although she now lives in California, she was then and had been for a long time a resident of Alabama. In her late twenties, she is married to a professional musician and is herself a licensed practical nurse. The Anglins have one son and are a happy well-adjusted couple. What led me to accept Mrs. Anglin's amazing experiences for inclusion in *Born Again* was the way in which she described her very first memories of coming back into this physical world. These descriptions were not only precise and detailed but matched pretty closely similar descriptions obtained by me from widely scattered sources. It is a scientific axiom that parallel reports from people who have no contact with each other and who cannot draw upon a joint source of information should be accepted at face value. Her reincarnation memories go back to the very moment of her most recent birth. She recounted her earliest experiences in this lifetime to her mother at a time when the little girl could not possibly have had this knowledge. We have her mother's testimony of the validity of this statement. As Nancy Anglin grew up her talents in the field of extrasensory perception grew with her. All through the years she had visions, clairvoyance, and other forms of extrasensory perception.

Soon after she moved to Montgomery in September of 1965 she noticed a vacant old house standing on South Court Street. Every time she passed the house she felt herself drawn to it for some unknown reason, but she did not give in to this urge until the summer of 1968. Finally she mustered enough courage to enter the dilapidated old house. It was on a Friday afternoon in May of 1968. Her husband and she were with a group of friends at the Maxwell Air Force Base Noncommissioned Officers Club. As is often the case, the conversation turned to haunted houses, and Mrs. Anglin mentioned the one she knew on Court Street. No sooner was this mentioned than the little group decided they all wanted to visit a haunted house. Mr. Anglin, however, decided to stay behind. The rest of the group piled into their convertible and drove to the house. The group included Sergeant and Mrs. Eugene Sylvester, both in their late thirties; Sergeant and Mrs. Bob Dannly, in their mid-thirties; and a Mrs. Harvey Ethridge, age thirty-five, the wife of another member of the 604th Band Squadron. The whole thing seemed like a lark to the group. But when they arrived behind the house Mrs. Dannly changed her mind and decided to wait in the car. The rest of them walked up along the shaded back drive around the left side of the house and entered it through the front door. Since the house was vacant it was also unlocked. They walked through the hall into the sitting room to their right. As soon as the group had entered that particular room Nancy Anglin became extremely alert and the hair on her arms stood up. Sergeant Dannly noticed her strange state and immediately asked her if there was anything wrong. While the others went on, she and Sergeant Dannly remained behind in this room for a few minutes. Both noticed that the temperature suddenly dropped and that there was an undefinable feeling of another presence about. They knew at once that they were not alone.

Since the others had gone on to other rooms they decided to join them in the rear of the house. Near the back stairs by the kitchen door they discovered, scattered on the floor, old Veterans of Foreign War records that seemed to have been there for a long time. Eagerly they picked up some of the papers and started to read them aloud to each other. As they did so they clearly heard the sound of a small bell. They perked their ears and the sound was heard once again. Immediately they started to look all over the first floor of the house. Nowhere was there a bell. Since both of them had clearly heard the bell they knew that they had not hallucinated it. But as their search for the bell had proven fruitless, they decided to leave by the front door. They had gone only a few steps when Sergeant Sylvester cried out in excitement. At his feet lay an old magazine illustrated with a figure pointing a finger and a caption reading "Saved by the Bell." This seemed too much of a coincidence for them, so they picked up the magazine and went back into the house. Both sergeants and Nancy Anglin went back into the area where they had heard the mysterious bell. After a moment of quiet they heard it again. As they questioned the origin of the bell and spoke about it the sound became louder and louder. Needless to say they could not find any source for the ringing and eventually they left the house.

Now Nancy Anglin's curiosity about the house was aroused. The following Sunday she returned to the vacant house, this time armed with a camera and flash bulbs. Again she searched the house from top to bottom for any possible source for the sound of a small bell. Again there was nothing that could have made such a sound. At that point she felt a psychic urge to photograph the staircase where the bell had first been heard. Using a good camera and a setting of infinity and exposing 1/60th of a second at 5.6 on Ektachrome-X color film rated at ASA 64, she managed to produce a number of slides. It was late evening, so she used blue flash bulbs to support the natural light. However, there were no reflective surfaces or odd markings on the wall. Nevertheless, upon examining the developed slides she found that two faces appeared on one of the slides. One seems to be the outline of the head and shoulders of a man and the second one seems to be the face of a woman with her hair piled high on her head and a scarf loosely tied around her shoulders. Nancy Anglin went back to the haunted house many times and heard the bell on several occasions. Others had heard it too. Marion Foster, at the time the Montgomery County Job Corps

Director, and Charles Ford, a graduate student in psychology at Auburn University, are among those who heard the bell.

The house in question was known as the Ray-Branch Home. According to Milo Howard, Director of the Alabama State Archives, the house was built in 1856 by a Scottish gentleman by the name of Ray. After the turn of the century the house was sold to the Branch family, who altered the appearance by adding six stately Corinthian columns in front. A member of the Branch family confirmed that their family had lived there for twenty years, after which time the home had been sold to the Veterans of Foreign Wars to be used as state headquarters. Despite diligent search by Nancy Anglin and her librarian friends, nothing unusual could be turned up pertaining to any tragic event in the house. But the records of the middle nineteenth century are not complete and it is entirely possible that some tragic event did take place of which we have no knowledge. Unfortunately the house has recently been demolished and replaced by a motel on the new Interstate Highway 65.

But Nancy had other psychic experiences in Alabama. Prior to her marriage she lived at 710 Cloverdale Road in Montgomery in an old house divided into four apartments, two downstairs and two upstairs. She occupied the upstairs east apartment alone for six months prior to her marriage. When she first moved in, she became immediately aware of an extraordinary presence. After her new husband moved in with her this became even stronger. Her first definite experience took place in August of 1966 around three o'clock in the morning. At the time she was sitting alone in her living room when she heard the sound of a flute playing a wandering mystical pattern of notes. Surprised at this, she looked up and saw a pink mist approaching from the bedroom where her husband was then sleeping. The mist crossed the living room and entered the den. As the cloud floated out, the music also died off. Since her husband is a professional musician and she herself is very interested in singing, this manifestation was of particular importance to her, although she could not understand its meaning.

Soon enough she had another experience. This time she was entirely alone in the big old house when the living-room door began to vibrate with the sound of footsteps. Quivering with fear, she sat while the feet walked up and down in an almost impatient manner. Finally mustering up enough courage she commanded the noise to stop. Whatever was causing the footsteps obeyed her command, because for a few minutes all was quiet. Then it started up again. Paralyzed with fear she was just sitting there when she heard her downstairs neighbor return home. It seemed to her as if an eternity had passed. Quickly she ran downstairs and rang his bell and asked him to come up and see what he could find about the mysterious footsteps. The neighbor's arrival did not interfere with the ghost's determination to walk up and down, it soon appeared. "Someone's walking around in here," explained the somewhat perplexed neighbor. As if to demonstrate her earlier success Nancy commanded the unseen walker to stop. Sure enough the footsteps stopped. Shaking his head the neighbor left, and the footsteps resumed. Finally coming to terms with the unseen visitor, Nancy tried to keep occupied until her husband returned at two o'clock in the morning. As soon as her husband returned they ceased abruptly. Evidently the ghost didn't mind the neighbor but did not want any trouble with a husband. The Anglins never did find out who the ghostly visitor was, but it seemed strange to them to have come to live in an old house where a musician had lived before them since both of them were so much involved with music themselves. Quite possibly the unseen gentleman himself had manipulated things so that they could get the apartment.

For some unknown reason a certain spot in Alabama has become a psychic focal point for Nancy Anglin. That spot is where the O'Neil Bridge crosses from the city of Sheffield to Florence, Alabama. Many years ago she had astral journeys that took her in flight across that bridge during its construction. She remembers the sensational feeling and wondering whether she would make it across or fall to her death. In that dream she clearly saw planks in a crosswalk high above the water and had the feeling of being pursued by some menacing individual. In the dream she looked down upon the water, became dizzy and then saw nothing further. The O'Neil Bridge was built before her birth. Every time she has had to cross it in reality Nancy Anglin has had to suppress a great fear about it. In her childhood she had a firm belief that the bridge would eventually collapse and pull her to her death. This despite the fact that it is a sturdy bridge constructed of concrete and steel.

In the fall of 1968 she began having a recurrent dream in which she drove across the O'Neil Bridge from Sheffield to Florence, then took a left turn and traveled down along the river and rode a long distance until she reached a massive stone house that stood four stories tall. In her vision she spent the night on the third floor of that house. She was visited by a rather fierce female spirit possessed of a resounding voice. With that she awoke.

On December 27, 1968, Nancy Anglin visited some friends on the far side of Florence, Alabama. The conversation turned to haunted houses, stately mansions and such, and the friends offered to show her an old house they had recently discovered. The group traveled over a series of back roads until they reached a large gray sandstone house standing four stories tall and overlooking the Tennessee River. The house was vacant and the interior had been destroyed long ago by treasure seekers. The stairs leading up to the third floor were torn down. Nancy was fascinated by the house and decided to visit it again on New Year's Day. This time, however, she traveled in the same direction as she had done in her dream, but she had not yet realized that it was the same house. Somehow the house seemed familiar, but she did not connect this particular house with the one in her recurrent dream. Finally in another dream on the 21st of March of that year she realized that the house was one and the same as the one in her dream vision. Now she found herself on the third floor of the house in a large room containing a chaise longue of an earlier period. She had lain down to rest when she heard a booming angry voice on the floor above her. Then as if blown by a strong wind came an apparition from the fourth floor. She could see a face, that of a white woman with narrow features, angry as she said something in a vibrating, commanding voice. The noise of this voice awoke her. A few weeks later the dream repeated itself. By now Nancy Anglin knew the name of the house, Smithsonia. Then in early March of 1969 she dreamed a variation in which she saw herself on the third floor. Again the forceful female spirit appeared and screamed at her. This time she could make out the words "Get out, Get out!" Subsequently Nancy found herself standing on the grounds with a group of people watching the house go up in flames while a deafening voice raged from within the burning structure. At that she awoke suddenly. Only later in the day did she realize that the house in her dream had been the Smithsonia. On the night of March 29th she awoke to hear a ringing in her ears. Her body was tingling all over as if her circulation had stopped. She felt herself weighted down by some tremendous force and could neither move nor breathe. While her conscious mind seemed to be ascending above herself all she could do was think how to get back into her body and a state of normalcy. After what seemed like an eternity she felt herself catch a deep gulping breath and her senses returned.

In late April she returned home for a visit and was informed that Smithsonia had burned down about three weeks before. The day of the fire matched her last terrifying experience. Was there any connection between the fierce spirit in the burning house and herself and was Nancy Anglin reliving something from her own past, or was she merely acting as the medium for some other tortured soul? At any rate Smithsonia stands no more.

I am indebted to Mrs. H. L. Stevens of Foley, Alabama, for two interesting psychic cases. Mrs. Stevens is a retired schoolteacher in her sixties and a careful observer of facts. Since she has had an interest in ESP since childhood and has had various minor experiences with psychic occurrences herself, she has been an unofficial counselor to those who come to seek her advice and who cannot cope with their own psychic experiences. A fellow teacher whose initials are M. B. had just lost her husband. Reluctantly she sold her house and most of the furnishings. The following night, very tired and unhappy, she went to bed early. As a mathematics instructor she was not given to hallucinations or idle dreams. As she lay in bed unable to fall asleep she thought over the plans for the delivery of the furniture that had been sold and the disposition of some of the articles that no one had purchased. At the foot of her bed was a dresser on which stood a musical powder box. This was a special gift from her late husband. Suddenly as she lay there the music box began to play of its own volition. Mrs. B. was terrified, believing that someone had gotten into the room and had knocked the lid of the music box aside. That was the only way in which the box could be activated. The music box played the entire tune and Mrs. B. lay there stiff with fear, expecting someone at any moment to approach the bed. Then there was an interval, perhaps a minute or two, and the music box began again, playing the entire tune as if it had been rewound, although no one approached the bed. After what seemed like an eternity to her she arose and turned on the light. There was no one in the room. The lid was in its proper place on the box. All the doors in the house were locked. There was no way in which the music box could have played of its own accord. Mrs. B. knew then that her late husband wanted her to know he still cared. Somehow this last greeting made things a lot easier for her the next morning.

Warren F. Godfrey is an educated man who works for the NASA Center in Houston. He and his wife Gwen had no particular interest in the occult and were always careful not to let their imagination run away with them. They lived in a house in Huntsville, Alabama, which was, at the time they moved into it, only three years old. At first they had only a feeling that *the house didn't want them.* There was nothing definite about this, but as time went on they would look over their shoulders to see if they were being followed, and felt silly doing so. Then, gradually, peculiar noises started. Ordinarily such noises would not disturb them, and they tried very hard to blame the settling of the house. There were cracks in the ceiling, the popping and cracking of corners, then the walls would join in, and after a while there would be silence again. Faucets would start to drip for no apparent reason. Doors would swing open and/or shut by themselves, and a dish would shift in the cupboard. All these things could perhaps have been caused by a house's settling, but the noises seemed to become organized. Warren noticed that the house had a definite atmosphere. There seemed to be a feeling that the house objected to the young couple's happiness. It seemed to want to disturb their togetherness in whatever way it could, and it managed to depress them.

Then there were knockings. At first these were regularly spaced single sharp raps proceeding from one part of the house to another. Warren ran out and checked the outside of the house, under it, and everywhere and could discover no reason for the knocks. As all this continued they became even more depressed and neither liked to stay alone in the house. About Thanksgiving of 1968 they went to visit Warren's mother in Illinois for a few days. After they returned to the empty house it seemed quieter, even happier. Shortly before Christmas, Warren had to go to Houston on business. While he was gone Gwen took a photograph of their daughter Leah. When the picture was developed there was an additional head on the film, with the face in profile and wearing some sort of hat. Warren, a scientist, made sure that there was no natural reason for this extra face on the film. Using a Kodak Instamatic camera with a mechanism that excludes any double exposure, he duplicated the picture and also made sure that a reflection could not have caused the second image. Satisfied that he had obtained sufficient proof to preclude a natural origin for the second face on the film, he accepted the psychic origin of the picture.

About that time they began hearing voices. One night Warren woke up to hear two men arguing in a nearby room. At first he dismissed it as a bad dream and went back to sleep, but several nights later the same thing happened. After listening to them for a while he shrugged his shoulders and went back to sleep. He could not understand a word they were saying but was sure that there were two men arguing. After several weeks of this his wife also heard the voices. To Warren this was gratifying since he was no longer alone in hearing them. The time when both of them heard the voices was generally around 1 a.m. In addition to the two men arguing Gwen has also heard a woman crying and Warren has heard people laughing. The noises are not particularly directed toward them, nor do they feel that there is anything evil about them. Gradually they have learned to ignore them. As a trained scientist Warren tried a rational approach to explain the phenomena but could not find any cause. Turning on the lights did not help either. The phenomena occurred only in the master bedroom. There are no television stations on the air at that time of the morning and there is no house close enough for human voices to carry that far. In trying to reach for a natural explanation Warren considered the fact that caves extended underneath the area, but what they were hearing was not the noise of rushing waters. Those were human voices and they were right there in the room with them. They decided to learn to live with their unseen boarders and perhaps the ghosts might eventually let them in on their "problem." Not that Warren and Gwen could do much about them, but it is always nice to know what your friends are talking about, especially when you share your bedroom with them.

Mary Carol Henry is in her early thirties, lives in Montgomery and is married to a medical technician in the USAF. She is the mother of seven children and has had psychic experiences from early childhood. When Mary was twelve years old one of her older brothers moved to Pittsburgh. She lent a helping hand with the furniture and other belongings and decided to stay overnight so she could help them finish up the work early in the morning. The house was an old four-story one in the Hazelwood section of Pittsburgh. Mary and the children slept up on the third floor, but she felt very uneasy about staying. Somehow the house bothered her. Since she had promised to stay overnight, however, she went to bed around 10 p.m. and lay in bed for a while thinking about why the house had troubled her. Her brother's baby slept in the same room with her and after a while her brother came up to check on the child. She then heard him go back downstairs. Mary wasn't sure how much time had elapsed when she thought she heard him come up again. There was the rustling of newspapers or something that sounded like it, and she assumed it was her brother, since he was in the habit of taking a newspaper with him when he went to the bathroom. She turned over, and instead of her brother, to her amazement she saw a young girl come out of a closet. Immediately she recognized her as her little sister Patsy who had been killed in a gas explosion in August of 1945 at the age of five. The ghost wore the same gown she had been buried in and she looked exactly as she had when she was alive but somehow larger in build. Her apparition was enveloped by a green light. As Mary stared in disbelief the ghost came over to the bed and sat on the side of it. Mary saw the bed actually sink in where Patsy sat on it. Her sister then put her hands on Mary's and kissed her on the cheek. Mary felt the kiss as if it were the kiss of a living person. Then the apparition vanished. Still dazed with fear, Mary sprang out of bed and spent the rest of the night on the stairs. When she told her experience to her mother later, her mother assured her that her late sister had only come back to comfort her in what must have been unfamiliar surroundings, for if Mary was to see a ghost that night it might just as well be someone in the family, not a stranger.

ARKANSAS

Hollygrove is only a small town in eastern Arkansas, but to Sharon Inebnit it is the center of her world. She lives there with her farmer husband in quiet rural Arkansas far from metropolitan centers. Little Rock is a long way off and not a place one is likely to visit often. Her mother lives in Helena close to the Mississippi state line. Traveling east on Highway 86 and then on 49 Sharon has gone back and forth a few times in her young life. She knows the area well. It is not an area of particular merit but it has one advantage: it's very quiet. About halfway between Hollygrove and Helena stands an old house that attracted Sharon every time she passed it. There was no reason for it, and yet whenever she passed the old house something within her wondered what the house's secret was.

Sharon is now in her early twenties. She has lived with an extraordinary gift of ESP since infancy. That is a subject one doesn't discuss freely in her part of the world. People either ridicule you or, worse, think you're in league with the devil. So Sharon managed to keep her powers to herself even though at times she couldn't help surprising people. She would often hear voices of people who weren't even within sight. If she wanted someone to call her, all she had to do was visualize the person and, presto, the person would ring her. Whenever the telephone rings she knows exactly who is calling. Frequently she has heard her neighbors talking 500 yards from her house, yet she is so sensitive she cannot stand the television when it is turned on too loud.

Her husband, a farmer of Swiss extraction, is somewhat skeptical of her powers. He is less skeptical now than he was when he first met her. Back in the summer of 1963 when she and her present husband first kept company she was already somewhat of a puzzle to him. One day, the fifteen-year-old girl insisted they drive into Helena, which was about five miles from where they were then. Her boyfriend wanted to know why. She insisted that there was a baseball game going on and that a private swimming party was in progress at the municipal pool. She had no reason to make this statement, however, nor any proof that it was correct, but they were both very much interested in baseball games, so her boyfriend humored her and decided to drive on to Helena. When they arrived at Helena they found that a baseball game was indeed going on and that a private swimming party was in progress at the municipal pool just as Sharon had said. Helena has a population of over 10,000 people. Sharon lives 25 miles away. How could she have known this?

In March of 1964 her maternal grandmother passed away. She had been close to her but for some reason was unable to see her in her last moments. Thus the death hit her hard and she felt great remorse at not having seen her grandmother prior to her passing. On the day of the funeral she was compelled to look up, and there before her appeared her late grandmother. Smiling at her, she nodded and then vanished. But in the brief moment when she had become visible to Sharon the girl understood what her grandmother wanted her to know. The message was brief. Her grandmother understood why she had not been able to see her in her last hours and wanted to forgive her.

In April of 1964 when she was just sixteen years old she married her present husband. They went to Memphis, Tennessee, for four days. All during their honeymoon Sharon insisted on returning home. She felt something was wrong at home even though she couldn't pinpoint it. Though it wasn't a hot period of the year she felt extremely warm and very uncomfortable. Eventually her husband gave in to her urgings and returned home with her. Assuming that her psychic feelings concerned an accident they might have on the road, she insisted that they drive very carefully and slowly. There was no accident. However, when they entered the driveway of her home she found out what it was she felt all that distance away. A large fertilizer truck had hit a gasoline truck in front of her mother's house. A tremendous fire had ensued, almost setting her mother's house on fire. The blaze could be seen clearly in towns over 5 miles away. Both trucks burned up completely. It was the heat from the fire she had felt all the way to Memphis, Tennessee.

The house outside of Hollygrove, however, kept on calling her and somehow she didn't forget. Whenever she had a chance to drive by it she took it, looking at the house and wondering what its secret was. On one such occasion it seemed to her that she heard *someone play a piano inside the vacant house.* But that couldn't very well be; she knew that there was no one living inside. Perhaps there were mice jumping up and down the keyboard, if indeed there was a piano inside the house. She shook her head, dismissing the matter. Perhaps she had only imagined it. But somehow the sound of songs being played on an old piano kept on reverberating in her mind. She decided to do some research on the house.

Tom Kameron runs an antique shop in Hollygrove, and since the old house was likely to be filled with antiques he would be the man to question about it. That at least was Sharon's opinion. She entered the shop pretending to browse around for antiques. A lady clerk came over and pointed at an old lamp. "I want to show you something that you'll be interested in," she said. "This came from the old Mulls house here." Sharon was thunderstruck. The Mulls house was the house she was interested in. She began to question the clerk about the antiques in the Mulls house. Apparently a lot of them had been stolen or had disappeared during the last few years. Since then a caretaker had been appointed who guarded the house. At this point the owner of the shop, Tom Kameron, joined the conversation. From him Sharon learned that the house had belonged to Tom Mulls, who had passed away, but Mrs. Mulls, although very aged, was still alive and living in a sanitarium in Little Rock. Kameron himself had been a friend of the late owners for many years.

The house had been built by a Captain Mulls who had passed away around 1935. It was originally built in St. Augustine, Florida, and was later moved to Hollygrove.

The captain wasn't married, yet there was a woman with him in the house when it stood in Hollygrove. This was an Indian girl he had befriended and who lived with him until her death. The man who later inherited the house, Tom Mulls, was an adopted son. Apparently Captain Mulls was very much in love with his Indian lady. After her death he had her body embalmed and placed in a glass casket which he kept in a room in the house. It stayed there until he died, and when Tom took over the house he buried the casket in the cemetery not far away. Her grave still exists in that cemetery. There were many Indian relics and papers dealing with Indian folklore in the house during her lifetime but they have all disappeared since. The Indian girl played the piano very well indeed and it was for her that the captain had bought a very fine piano. Many times he would sit listening to her as she played song after song for his entertainment.

The house has been vacant for many years but people can't help visiting it even though it is locked. They go up to the front steps and peer in the windows. Sharon was relieved to hear that she was not the only one strangely attracted to the old house. Others have also been "called" by the house as if someone inside were beckoning to them. Over the years strangers who have passed by the house have come to Mr. Kameron with strange tales of music emanating from the empty house. What people have heard wasn't the rustling of mice scurrying over a ruined piano keyboard but definite tunes, song after song played by skilled hands. Eventually the house will pass into the hands of the state since Mrs. Mulls has no heirs. But Sharon doubts that the ghost will move out just because the house changes hands again. She feels her presence, very much alive and wholly content to live on in the old house. True, she now plays her songs to a different kind of audience than she did when Captain Mulls was still alive, but then it is just possible that the captain has decided to stay behind also if only to listen to the songs his Indian lady continues to play for his entertainment.

FLORIDA

Dr. Rebekah Parker is a long-time resident of Fort Myers. She has taken the occult matter-of-factly all her life, neither being afraid nor shying away from it because of her position. That is because she has had experiences herself. Experiences that can't be explained on so-called rational grounds. Many years ago she was in charge of a children's home in another state. When she took the position she was assigned a certain room. The room seemed cheerful enough at first. Soon, however, she realized that there was something terribly wrong with it. Almost from the start of her residence there she would awake around three o'clock in the morning with the definite impression that someone was trying to choke her. The strange sensation was not of her own doing, she realized; there was nothing physically wrong with her. While she considered asking for another room and at the same time dismissing such a request as outlandish and probably out of place, she also realized that something had to be done about the situation.

One day the grandmother of one of the children under her care called on her and engaged her in conversation. Although the doctor had not brought up the subject, somehow the conversation veered toward the occult. The lady avowed freely that she was psychic. Dr. Parker decided she should test the lady's abilities and she asked her whether she could tell her anything about the room they were in. The lady nodded and closed her eyes and leaned back in the chair. Almost instantly the woman went through the movements of someone being choked to death. In front of the doctor's surprised eyes the woman turned purple in the face and had all she could do to break the spell which had suddenly come on her for no apparent physical or logical reason. As soon as she had regained control over herself she explained what had happened. A bride of six months had been choked to death by her husband in that very room.

Dr. Parker demanded proof and details. Again the lady medium closed her eyes and came up with names and dates. How she could have known so much about the house was a mystery since she had not been in it before. "What shall I do about this?" the doctor asked. "The husband is earthbound," the lady medium said and suggested that the doctor pray for him. Prayer might very well release him. The doctor nodded and thanked the lady for her help. The following night she prayed in earnest until three o'clock. She had prepared herself for this, determined to rid her room once and for all from its evil connotations. At the stroke of three a figure appeared before her. It was a male wearing what seemed like a long nightshirt and a stocking cap on his head. The doctor did not panic but remained in her bed praying. She observed how the figure passed through the open door and walked down the stairs in his bare feet. She could plainly hear the noise of the feet touching the floor. Then she heard him open the front door and disappear into the rose garden in back of the house. Never again did Dr. Parker have the choking experience from that moment on.

She asked the lady who had given her the key to the psychic experiences in the room to return to the home to inform her of her own experiences. Was the unhappy man really gone? Again the medium leaned back and closed her eyes. She could still see him in the garden at night, she explained, but he was no longer earthbound and could leave at will.

Mrs. Alverna Allender lives at West Panama City Beach, Florida. She is a lady in her middle years with grown children and comes from a family where ESP experiences have been frequent. Probably the most unusual experience she has had happened one day in 1965 when she lived in Kenner, Louisiana. She was waiting for the bus with her four-year-old son when suddenly she felt herself traveling at great speed in the direction of the house of a church member whom she knew and who lived about seven miles away from her. She could see the landscape flying by as if she were traveling on a very fast bus. She was nearly there when she turned around and looked back toward where she had come from. At that point she felt her four-year-old pull her leg saying, "Mommy, the bus is coming." She found herself back at the bus stop. She did not experience any sensation of riding back to the bus stop. One moment she was near a friend's house, the next moment back at the bus stop. She felt somewhat odd but otherwise all right.

All week long she tried to puzzle out her strange experience. About a week after the occurrence had taken place she ran into a friend by the name of Helen Kenner. Agitated, her friend stopped her on the street. "Hey," she said. "Are you haunting me?" Mrs. Allender demanded to know what this was all about. Patiently Helen Kenner explained that she had been in her trailer home a week before when she had seen her standing outside looking in. Immediately she had told her husband that they were going to have a visitor and to put his shirt back on, for it had been a very warm evening. When she turned around and looked out the window the apparition of her friend was gone. She ran outside to look, assuming that her friend had just wandered off for a moment and would enter the house almost immediately, but there was no one around. Mrs. Allender demanded to know what she had looked like and what kind of clothes she was wearing at the time. Without a moment's hesitation Helen Kenner answered, "A pink blouse and a blue skirt."

Mrs. Allender blanched. The description of her dress was entirely correct. Moreover, she had made that pink print blouse herself, had never worn it before and thus her friend could not have seen it on a prior occasion.

Carolyn Manning comes from Miami, Florida, though she now lives in Ohio. She has had ESP experiences all her life but the experience that shook her up the most happened to her not long ago. For several nights she dreamed an identical dream. In this dream a casual friend of hers whom we shall refer to as Mrs. B. called her and asked her to come to her house. In the dream Carolyn went to her friend's house and looked at a cold spot in the den. Her friend had asked her to come over and help her figure out why a certain spot was always so cold. The spot, her friend explained, was so cold she could not even put a chair into it. Next Carolyn saw herself walking up to a patio with sliding doors and had the feeling of gravel under her feet. Then she stepped up one step into a den and could plainly see the wooden panels. Now her friend showed her the cold spot and she reached out and felt the cold air herself. Suddenly she was drawn into that cold spot and felt herself coming out of her own body as if someone else were trying to take over her body. Immediately she knew that it was a young woman and that she was crying very hard. The entity said that she did not know where she was and kept calling for someone named Capp, over and over calling for Capp to help her. The words Carolyn heard in her dream were "Capp, Capp, please come and help me. I am lost. It is dark and I cannot see any more. Please, Capp. Please come and help me." Still in the dream, she heard herself ask the woman's name and was told it was Elaine or something close to that.

At that point the dream ended abruptly and Carolyn Manning found herself back in her own bed sitting up shaking and crying. She didn't feel that she had dreamed this but somehow that it had happened to her in reality. The impression was so strong it didn't leave her for days. Finally, after thinking it over, she decided to check on it. She hesitated to call her friend, a casual acquaintance, out of fear of being ridiculed, but she kept on having the same dream over and over. Finally it got to be too much and she decided to telephone the lady in question. Mrs. B. listened quietly as Carolyn Manning told her, in a haunting voice, what she had dreamed. When she had finished there was a moment of silence on the other end of the line.

Then Mrs. B. said that she did have a cold spot in her den and that the description given by Carolyn was entirely correct, yet Carolyn Manning had never been to Mrs. B.'s house and had no way of knowing what it looked like. As for the sobbing woman Elaine, or something close to that, and her crying out for Capp, Mrs. B. had an answer for that too. Capp was her husband's uncle. He had been married to a woman named Ellen who had died suddenly two months before.

The ways of the unseen are strange at times. Someone "out there" had evidently decided to have Carolyn serve as go-between bridging the gulf between a distraught and confused spirit and a husband who would want to know that his wife was still alive in another dimension.

GEORGIA

The state of Georgia, especially the area around Atlanta, is full of people interested in psychic research. Whether this has something to do with the fact that many cases exist in the area, or whether this is simply because Georgia has some fine universities and metropolitan centers where the interest in ESP has been high for many years, is hard to tell. But the fact is that I get far more cases of interest from the area of Atlanta and of Georgia in general than, for instance, Mississippi or Louisiana. The caliber of the people who have most of the experiences or are possessed of ESP talents is also quite high. A.W.C., a science teacher from rural Georgia, says he does not believe in ghosts as such; however, he is quick to admit that the experiences he has had will admit of no explanation other than a psychic one. When he was a teenager he was very close to his grandmother even though she lived 150 miles away.

One night, while he was in bed, he awoke and saw his grandmother standing in the corner of his room. At first he thought he was imagining things. He closed his eyes and looked once again but she was still there. Now he covered his head and after a while looked back; grandmother was still standing there. At that point he heard footsteps in the kitchen and got up to see if anybody had entered the kitchen, but to his surprise he found no one there. When he returned to his bedroom he decided, in his logical mind, that what he had seen had been a dress or some other piece of material hanging on the wall and not his grandmother. In the morning he would make sure that that was so. Came the morning and he checked and there was nothing in the corner of that room. However, a few days later the family received a telegram advising them that grandmother had had a stroke and was at the point of death. Evidently the young man had seen a projected image of his dear relative at a time when partial dissolution had taken place. Shortly thereafter the grandmother died.

But Mr. C. not only has been the recipient of psychic impressions, he has also been able to send them, although not at will. During World War II he was with the Army in France. His family frequently discussed his fate abroad. One evening his wife, sister, and an aunt who had reared him and who was particularly close to the young man were sitting in front of a wooden stove in their home. Suddenly the aunt started to scream. Terror-stricken, the woman explained that she had just seen Mr. C.'s face appear to her in the flames of the stove. At that very moment Mr. C. was wounded in France.

Robert Mullinax of Atlanta, Georgia, is in his early twenties. When he was seventeen years old, in 1967, he had an experience he will never forget. His mother had often had premonitions of things to come and perhaps some of this talent had come down to him also. On that particular day in April, Mrs. Mullinax had been very restless all day long as if something were about to happen. She had the feeling she should telephone her sister-in-law, but somehow she never got around to it. They were not particularly close; in fact, they had visited each other only about three times in twenty-five years. That evening she knew why she had had the strange feeling of urgency to call her sister-in-law. The woman had committed suicide by shooting herself.

It was two days after her death when young Robert found himself standing in his home in front of a large mirror. This was in their living room and he was about to comb his hair when he saw his aunt in the mirror behind him. He turned around and, sure enough, there she was standing about six feet away. As he got a closer look at her she vanished. In this fleeting moment young Robert had the impression that his aunt wanted to tell him something—perhaps express regret at what she had done and to send a message to her youngest son whom she loved very much, but she was gone before Robert could really make out the message. What is interesting about this case is the fact that the ghost was solid enough to be seen in a mirror, not merely a hallucination or a subjective vision.

Mrs. W. is a housewife living in Athens, Georgia. She is also a certified nursery school teacher, the mother of six children, and she has had ESP experiences for many years past. She is living proof that ESP messages can be very precise at times in giving the recipient an indication of what the message is all about and to prepare the recipient for any shock that might come his or her way. In 1946 Mrs. W. was living in another city in Georgia. At that time she had one son age two and a half years and another six months old. She was also pregnant with another child. During that period she had many vivid dreams of a psychic nature. But after the third child was born she was particularly disturbed one night by a dream which became so powerful that it awoke her. She found herself crying uncontrollably, so much so that her husband was genuinely concerned. When she became calmer she told her husband she had dreamed she saw her brothers and sisters and her mother looking at her through the glass of their front door, saying, "Call an ambulance." The dream had no meaning for her, so after a while she went back to sleep and didn't think about it again. Three months later the dream became a reality. Her brother appeared at her front door and standing outside the glass said, "Call an ambulance." He then explained that their father, who lived on the next street and who had no telephone, had suffered a heart attack while preparing for bed. The father died three days later. It was only after her grief ceased that Mrs. W. realized that in her dream she had seen all members of her family except one—her father was not in it. Had she understood this properly perhaps she would have been more prepared for the shock that was to come her way shortly.

The relationship with her father had been a close one, so she was not surprised that after his passing there were times when she felt him standing near her. She did not see him, yet she knew of his presence. She hesitated to discuss this with her husband out of fear of being ridiculed or worse. During that time she awakened her husband five or six separate times and asked him to get up and shut the door since Daddy had come in. Her husband didn't like it, but when she insisted he did get up in order to please his wife. They never discussed it until many years later when her husband admitted that each time she had asked him to close the door it was indeed open and there had been no reason for it to be open.

Mrs. W.'s husband is the editor of a county newspaper and a very logical man. He learned to accept his wife's special talent as the years rolled by, but there were times when he wished that she weren't as psychic as she was. One night she dreamed that a plane crash had taken place somewhere in back of their house and she saw some Army men drive up in a jeep and take away the bodies of those killed. In the morning she told her husband of this dream. He didn't say anything. Two weeks later, however, he told his wife to quit having "those crazy dreams." It appeared that Mr. W. had been traveling away from home in the direction one might properly call "back of the house" when he saw that an Army plane had crashed and Army personnel in a jeep had driven up to the site and removed some bodies, just as his wife had told him. Mrs. W. realized that she had a very special talent and perhaps had been chosen by some superior intelligence as a communicator.

A month after her daughter Karen was born in 1952 she happened to be lying down for an afternoon nap. She was facing the wall when she felt compelled to turn over in the opposite direction. There she saw the figure of a man in a white robe standing by her bed. Her first thought was that she still had in her system some of the drug that had been given her during the birth and that she was indeed hallucinating. She thought it best to turn back to the wall. Immediately, however, she felt a strong compulsion to turn back, and this time she saw the man pointing his finger at her with a stern look on his face. She got the impression she was to get up immediately and follow him. She did just that and walked straight into the next room. As if acting in a daze she saw herself dial her husband at his office. As soon as her husband came to the phone she told him not to ask questions but if he ever intended to do something that she had asked him for, this was the time to do it. She told him to go at once to a place called Curry's Creek to see if their son Joe was there. Her husband objected. He knew, he said, that the five-year-old was not there. Nevertheless Mrs. W. insisted. Her plea was so urgent she impressed her husband sufficiently that he did indeed go down to the creek. Ten minutes later he telephoned her asking her how she knew that the boy was indeed at the creek. It appeared that he had found the little boy on the edge of the water looking down into it. The creek furnishes the town's water supply and is next to a busy highway a mile outside of town. The child had never been there before. Had Mr. W. not arrived in time the child might very well have drowned. Mrs. W. then realized that the man in the white robe had come to save their child.

The warning of impending disaster is a recurrent theme in ghost lore. It appears that on occasion the departed are given the task of warning the living of impending difficulties or disaster but are not permitted to be specific. Evidently that would interfere with the exercise of free will under test conditions. A similar case involves a lady from Decatur by the name of Mrs. L. E., who, when a child, was staying with her Aunt Mary in her house. Twenty years before that visit Mary's Great-aunt Rev had passed on. With her cousins Mrs. E. then proceeded to one of the bedrooms in the house to fetch some of the tricycles they had stored in it to go outside and play. When they got to the door of the room they saw Great-aunt Rev standing in the middle of the room right where the tricycles were. She was looking at the children rather sternly. She wore her long white nightgown and her nightcap, the clothing she was wearing when she died. The children stood there transfixed by shock. They spoke her name more in fear than in reverence. Then they ran out. When they described the apparition to the owner of the house, Mrs. E.'s Aunt Mary was very solemn. "She came back," she said and began to move all the furniture from the house, taking it out into the yard away from the house. This seemed like strange behavior, but the children were young and did not understand many things. Then Aunt Mary took the children and walked with them up the road to a neighbor's house. There she left them. Several hours later when they returned they found the house had burned down to ashes. No one has seen the ghost of Aunt Rev since.

Tucker, Georgia, is about an hour's ride due north of Atlanta, a pleasant, almost suburban community populated by pleasant, average people. The Stevens house, a landmark as early as 1854, was built of huge hand-hewn chestnut pine logs originally. The older part was added to by a Baptist minister around 1910. Finally another addition was made to the house in the late 1940s. When the Stevenses bought the house they were told that it was originally built by Indian settlers in the area around 1800, or even before. This is Cherokee Territory and according to the local tradition the Indians brought their sick to this house. They would stay with them overnight on their way to Decatur. Decatur was the town where the famed Dr. Chapman Powell lived. The Powell cabin has been restored and is now located in Stone Mountain Park, but originally it was in Decatur and was moved to the park to better preserve it as a landmark. The Stevens house stands about a mile off the High Tower Trail, which is the old Cherokee Indian trail, and four miles from Stone Mountain Park. Since Mrs. Stevens is herself about one-thirty-second

Cherokee, she has a vivid sympathy for all Indian lore and has always been interested in the Indian background of her house. When they first bought the house in May of 1960 the Stevenses lived in it for only a year. Then, for business reasons, they moved down to Florida and sold their house to their in-laws. However, two years later they returned from Florida and bought the house back. During that first year in the house they do not recall anything strange except for a recurrent dream Mrs. Stevens had right from the start when they took up residence at the house. In that dream she saw herself looking up through an opening in the ceiling into the darkness of a loft. She could clearly make out the rafters, wooden beams, and the chimneys. Somehow this dream seemed all very familiar. As soon as she had moved to the house she realized that her dream visions concerned the attic of their house. It looked exactly like the visions she had seen so many years prior to coming to the house. Evidently it was predestined that the Stevenses should take up residence in Tucker. On recollection Mrs. Stevens remembers that her in-laws had no special experiences in the house out of the ordinary during the two years in which they resided there. But then neither of her in-laws professed any particular interest in the occult or was possessed of psychic sensitivities.

As soon as the Stevenses had returned to their original home they noticed a strange feeling, perhaps more of a current all around the house. It affected the children as well. They would not want to take a nap or go to bed because they said someone kept touching them. Soon Mrs. Stevens experienced that too. Their smallest child reported seeing a man on the porch when there was no man about. Both Mr. and Mrs. Stevens have seen a man going across the porch. This has happened a number of times. Sometimes it is only a kind of quick flash and sometimes they can clearly make out a human form. Whenever they have seen something and their children have not, they try their best to keep it from them so as not to alarm them. Nevertheless the children on their own report similar occurrences. Gradually it has become clear to the Stevenses that the oldest part of the house, the log part, is the center of the psychic phenomena. In the living room-dining room area they have seen a form when there was certainly no one else but themselves in the house. On another occasion Mrs. Stevens has seen a hand materialize by her bed. In August of 1968 Mr. Stevens awoke from sound sleep because he had the feeling that there was someone in the house who should not be there. He sat up and looked into the room where their sons were sleeping across from the parents' bedroom. There he saw a gray form standing by their bunkbeds looking at the oldest boy. Fully awake now, Mr. Stevens looked closely at the form and realized it was female. The woman appeared to be wearing a cowl-type hood. When he made a move the form dissolved into thin air. Stevens discussed the appearance with his wife. She had seen a similar form in the boys' room reclining on the lower bunk beside the youngest boy. Moreover, the apparition was not alone. Mrs. Stevens could make out additional figures in the room. Footsteps up and down the stairs when there was no one around to make them had become a common occurrence in the house. The Stevenses thought that the repair work going on in the house might have offended one or the other of its former inhabitants. They were doing their level best to save the old part of the house, repairing what could be repaired and replacing what could not.

It was soon clear to them that they had more than one unearthly visitor in their house. The woman so concerned with the well-being of the children might have been someone left behind from the Indian days or perhaps the shade of a former owner of the house. None of them ever saw her clearly enough to make sure, but there was someone else. In 1966 Mr. Stevens had a strange dream. The dream was followed by similar dreams, continuing, as it were, the narrative of the first one. In these dreams his brother Bill communicated with him. Bill had been killed in a plane crash in North Carolina during World War II. However, in the dreams Bill explained that he was not dead and that he had returned home. In another dream he wanted his brother to accompany him on a trip. In all of these dreams Bill appeared to have aged. He was balding and wearing a tattered officer's khaki uniform. His overcoat in particular was tattered and faded. While the Stevenses discussed these dreams with each other, they made a special point of never talking about them with their children. So the children had no idea that dreams about Uncle Bill had indeed taken place.

About three weeks after the last of this series of dreams involving Bill, all the boys came into the kitchen very much alarmed and white as sheets. They insisted that they had seen a ghost. When questioned about the apparition they said they had seen a man walk across the front room, which is part of the 1910 addition of the house. Immediately the parents checked to see whether a trespasser had perhaps entered the house. There was no one to be seen. Skeptical, and at the same time alarmed, the parents demanded that the boys describe what they had seen. Without a moment's hesitation they described the ghost as being a thin man, sort of crouched down and bald, with clothes rather torn and sort of a faded khaki. They did in effect describe exactly what Uncle Bill looked like in the series of dreams their father had had for so long. Only what they had seen was not in the dream state. Uncle Bill evidently had returned from the grave not as a resident ghost, for ghosts do not travel, but to look after the affairs of his brother's family.

Watkinsville is a small town of about five hundred people nine miles from the city of Athens and as quiet a place as you may want to visit. The people here are church-going, law-abiding citizens who have no interest in such things as psychic phenomena. The entire village consists of two streets. Where the street divides one takes the left fork and past the railroad track one arrives at a stately house that once belonged to the town doctor. Built around 1960, the house stands about a mile from the tracks surrounded by a good deal of land. The doctor had built the house for himself in his middle years, but after he moved in something happened with his wife. For some reason she started to drink, and not long after they had come to live in the house she committed suicide by shooting herself in the head. Two years later the doctor remarried. Something happened to his second wife as soon as they had settled in the house. She became addicted to drugs and could not find any rest even at night. The house was lit up all through the night until the doctor could no longer cope with his ill wife and had her committed to an asylum. The tragedies took their toll on the doctor, however, and not much later he died of an overdose of drugs. The verdict was death due to heart failure caused by an overdose of drugs. Evidently the doctor knew just how much to take.

After some litigation and questions about the property, the house and grounds were sold at public auction in Clarke County, passing into the hands of Mr. and Mrs. J. B. The young couple had two children. He was a mechanic, and psychic phenomena didn't interest him at all; in fact he firmly considered them just so much fantasy. Not so for his wife. Carol had known about the unseen world all her life. At the time when she was living with her grandmother, who was bringing her up, she had her first psychic experience. She was only eight years at the time but the memory is still as fresh with her now as if it had happened yesterday. She awoke in the middle of the night for no apparent reason. Then she felt a familiar hand on her shoulder. The hand belonged to her grandmother but it seemed icy cold. The next morning she reported the experience to her grandmother, who assured her that she had not touched the child. Soon after, her grandmother passed away. At the time when this happened Carol was holding her hand and the hand was ice cold.

She was about twenty years of age when she and her husband moved into the former doctor's house at Watkinsville. Soon after they had moved in she realized that they were not alone in the house. It was a very hot day and her older son was asking for a glass of water. After the boy had drunk the water Carol took the glass and placed it securely on a shelf inside the house, about halfway from either edge. When she started to leave the room again the glass flung itself to the floor and shattered completely. There was no logical explanation for this. After her husband returned home from work she told him what had happened. He did not believe in ghosts. That very evening her husband had finished a piece of cake and his wife took the plate and fork and placed it on the range in their kitchen. The range was in full view through the doorway of the living room. While her husband was watching television Carol was looking toward the range for reasons she did not know at the time. Suddenly she saw the plate lift itself off the range and fall to the floor with a resounding crash. Again there was no possible logical explanation since she had placed the plate well away from the edge of the range. There had been no earthquake or other movement of the house to account for the astonishing performance by the plate. Shortly thereafter she awoke at three-thirty in the morning because she heard a radio playing. Since she knew that the radio had been out of order for some time she got up and went to the bathroom to see whether there was a neighbor's radio playing. She realized that the radio was on in the garage. As she looked out the bathroom window she also saw that the dashboard light on the car was on and the radio playing full blast. Her first thought was that her husband had left the glove compartment open and the radio on. He assured her he had not. In fact he remembered clearly that he had turned the radio off and closed the glove compartment. He knew better than to turn the radio on when the car was in the garage since it played on the batteries when the motor was shut off. This was something a mechanic would never do. Having no explanation for the strange behavior of their car, they dismissed it. About a week later they were standing by their fence looking at the neighbor's house when the radio in their car started playing again by itself. They were standing just a few yards away and there was no possible way in which anyone could have entered the garage without being seen by them. At this point her husband went to the house to fetch a shotgun. Carol took her little son and returned to the house. Just as her husband approached the car with the shotgun the door of the glove compartment flew open of its own volition. Feverishly Mr. B. searched everywhere, but there was no one about. He checked for a short in the radio and inspected the latch on the glove compartment. Both checked out fine.

Since they had only rented the house it was easy for them to move on. They explained to the owner that their child had contracted a rash and that they felt the area was too full of pollen and it would be better if they went to live in another part of the state. But when they became familiar with the history of the house they realized that the doctor's two mad wives were still playing pranks. Perhaps it was only the second wife who always liked the lights on all night, but one can't be entirely sure. They may have met in the world beyond and become fast friends.

The first time I heard of Mr. James Arthur Williams's haunted house in Savannah, Georgia, was when the advertising manager of Citroën cars told me about it. Mr. Leach assured me that as far as haunted houses went his friend's really was the McCoy. Not only did it look like one, the phenomena in it were countless and the owner, Williams, a man of impeccable judgment and taste. Since we drive a Citroën and know that it represents not only the unusual but also quality, I assumed that Mr. Leach's judgment in matters of haunted houses might also be thus oriented. Before I could put his opinion of haunted houses to a test, however, I received a letter from one of my readers, a Mrs. Marjorie Bruce who lives in Savannah. The house had been in the morning news and she had taken the trouble of researching some of the reported phenomena for me.

The house in question is a five-story building with a good foundation and a wooden superstructure. On top of the slanting roof is a so-called widow's walk, a small platform near the chimney safeguarded by a wooden banister on all four sides. On the right side there is an entrance to the first floor of the house, which is actually two stories above ground. The strange occurrences may be due to the fact that the house was moved from its original location at 312 Bryan Street to its present location at 507 East St. Julian Street near Houston and Price. This happened in 1963 and the house survived the four-block ride rather well.

The house itself was built in 1796 by a planter from Sea Island, Georgia, as his town house. It was designed in so-called gambrel style, something not usually associated with the South, but the planter had come originally from Newport, Rhode Island, where this type of house is common. The present owner, James Arthur Williams, is a native Georgian and has lived in Savannah since 1952. He is a professional interior designer and a member of the American Institute of Designers as well as a dealer in eighteenth-century antiques. He is in his early forties and lives in the house alone. Prior to acquiring the house he had scant interest in the occult. Except for a minor ESP experience in a house across the street from the one he now lives in there was little to make him wonder about the spirit world. All that changed after he moved into the house on Julian Street. He knew, of course, that a man had hanged himself from a tall fourposter and that others had died in it over the years under strange conditions. But that holds true of many old houses, and Mr.Williams paid little attention to these traditions and legends. Soon he realized that he had bought more than an empty old house.

Around three in the morning he would awaken to the sound of footsteps very close to his bed. It sounded as if someone were walking on sand or broken glass. Williams immediately assumed that he had to deal with an intruder and asked what the man wanted. There was no answer. Then someone ran toward the bedroom door and crashed into an open closet. Immediately Williams got out of bed and walked to the adjoining library to turn on the light. There was no intruder. He could still hear the sound of feet walking on the floor, yet there was no man to be seen to whom the feet might conceivably belong.

While he was restoring the old house he and four friends were looking over the day's work in the interior of the house. Suddenly they heard what sounded like a group of workmen moving about upstairs. Immediately they searched the house, floor by floor, and found no one. They decided to go up to the roof and stand on the widow's walk. They had not encountered a single living soul on the way up. When they reached the top of the house they heard the identical noises below them this time.

Not much later Williams happened to be out of town when his friends decided to pay the strange house a visit on their own. Since they were well acquainted with the owner they felt they were not doing anything wrong by inspecting the house in his absence, especially as it had not yet been fully restored. As they were walking about the garden-floor level they heard noises above them. It sounded as if people were moving about. One of the men went upstairs to investigate and, if necessary, challenge the intruder. When he reached the top floor he felt as if he had just walked into a pool of cold water. He lost control over his bodily movements and felt himself being drawn into an unfinished chimney shaft which dropped about thirty feet into the basement. When the man did not return, his friends began to worry about him. They went up the stairs and found him on the floor, face up, trembling and completely disheveled. He had thrown himself to the floor to break what he considered an evil spell. That was enough to convince the three men to leave the house. They decided to await the owner before venturing further into what they now knew was a haunted house. A mutual friend had an apartment directly across from the haunted house and they decided to await Williams's return there. As they were seated discussing the unnerving experience they had just gone through they glanced across the street toward Williams's house. At that precise moment they all heard a woman scream in agony across the street. They were terrified and sat in silence. When the scream resounded once again one of the men ran outside and looked up at the haunted house. To his surprise he saw a tall dark-haired man wearing a white shirt and black bow tie standing at a third-floor window. His first thought was that perhaps Williams had returned unbeknownst to them and was looking down into the street. He was so sure of this that he decided to call out to his friends to greet the returning Williams. Williams, however, was not there. When he returned later that evening he assured them that he was not wearing a bow tie such as one of the men had seen.

On one occasion Mr. Williams had the company of a policeman on some police business. Both men distinctly heard loud crashing noises from the area of the room where there was a pipe organ. The room was on the fourth floor and the policeman immediately rushed up to see who the intruder was. When he reached the pipe-organ room both men saw the door to an adjacent storeroom open by itself and shut itself of its own volition. The policeman confidently assured Williams that the intruder must be in that other room. He turned the doorknob and found it locked. Only after the key had been inserted in the lock did the door open, yet both men had seen it open and shut itself. Finally Williams consulted with William G. Roll of the American Psychical Research Foundation of North Carolina, and Roll came and conducted a thorough investigation of the phenomena. He interviewed some twenty or thirty people who had personally witnessed these occurrences and others. They were people from all walks of life, ranging from masons and construction workers to college men and scientists and in age from seventeen to sixty. From the testimony of these witnesses Mr. Roll concluded that genuine psychic phenomena were indeed taking place in the old house.

Some of the witnesses have seen a gray-haired man wearing a gray suit and a white tie. He may only be one of the ghosts in residence at 507 East St. Julian Street. Whether the ghosts have become active because of the move from their customary site a few years ago and are trying to let the owner know they preferred the original site is a moot question. Ghosts don't like to travel because it destroys memories tied to specific occasions.

Mr. Williams does not encourage visitors. Despite its reputation as a haunted house he considers this his home and, in the tradition of his Anglo-Saxon forebears, also his castle. The house is called the Hampton Lilly Bridge House, and when last reported, both Mr. Williams and the ghostly boarders were still in residence.

LOUISIANA

Jean Hatton comes from a family in which the psychic has been in evidence for many generations. Precognitive dreams, clairvoyance, foreknowledge of events or places have been rampant on her mother's side of the family, and even as a pre-teenager Jean had some ESP experiences. Around forty years of age now, she and her husband live in the heart of New Orleans. She was a professional musician for a while and taught music in high school for five years. Her mother's family is Irish, Dutch, and Indian, while her father's side of the family came from Wales, England, and Ireland. Thus a predominance of Celtic elements in her background may be responsible for her readiness to accept the reality of psychic phenomena. At any rate when she moved from her childhood home in San Antonio, Texas, to New Orleans she made friends with a married couple living on Decatur Street in the French

Quarter. The very first time she tried to enter their apartment she almost tripped. She felt a kind of elastic force trying to keep her out as if she were not welcome. The house in which the couple's apartment was located was a very old house. That one and some of the adjoining ones were among the few that hadn't been destroyed in the fires so common in this part of town. At least two hundred years old, the house in question was one of the finest examples of colonial architecture.

Forcing her way through the invisible curtain, Jean then entered the apartment. She saw an old fireplace against one wall facing a bedroom door. The entrance was to the right. To the left were the living room and a long narrow room probably used as a pantry or wardrobe. The owner of the apartment tried to tell her that something very tragic had occurred in the apartment, but before he could do so Jean herself told him the story. How she could know this was as much a mystery to her as it was to her host. But she pointed at a clock and insisted that it would always stop at three o'clock in the morning because it was then that "something had happened." Before she knew what she was doing Jean found herself standing by the fireplace looking at the clock. Then she turned toward the door, resting her hands on the mantelpiece. She seemed to be wearing a white gown with full sleeves, probably a nightgown. At this moment she clearly heard steps. A door was opened and through it came the "wrong man." The man she saw now clairvoyantly was tall, had unruly gray hair and a deep-set type face. He wore a silk hat and black cape. She knew then that the woman was trying to express herself through her; that she had been stabbed where she stood and had fallen in front of the fireplace.

At this moment she came out of her semi-trance. It was all she could get, but her host assured her that the impression was not fantasy. He explained that he had seen just such a woman walk at night, her bloody hands crossed on her breasts. Both he and his wife had frequently heard the footsteps of someone coming up the stairs to their third-floor apartment. One night when Sheri, the wife, was home alone playing old English folk songs on her guitar she looked up and saw the two entities standing there in the door. She was not afraid so she kept on looking at them before they faded away.

It became clear to the owner of the apartment that something very drastic had occurred at a previous time. But they could not figure it out and learned to live with their spectral visitors. One day the husband was up in the attic, above their apartment, clearing up some flooring. To his horror he discovered two human skeletons underneath. Hastily closing the door to the attic behind him, he took the two skeletons and quietly buried them. He decided not to report the matter to the police after all since it might have been something that had occurred a long time ago and calling attention to it now might draw unfavorable publicity to himself and the house. From that moment the psychic phenomena stopped abruptly. But the owner of the apartment was not satisfied until he knew what had caused the two skeletons to be buried in so unusual a place as the attic of the apartment. He started to dig into the past of the house and asked questions around the area. As far as he could figure out, this is what happened. The woman in the nightgown had lived in the apartment, and once while she was waiting for her lover the door had opened and instead of her lover her husband had come through it. He had discovered the relationship and had come to kill her. After he had murdered her he in turn waited until the lover arrived and killed him too, then hid the bodies in the attic.

Silently the host handed Jean a knife to touch and psychometrize, that is to say read from it what could be gleaned of its past. As if she had been handed a glowing piece of coal she dropped it immediately. She could not touch it no matter how often she tried. The knife was an old knife of nondescript appearance, with a discolored blade, and of no particular merit. Almost hysterical, with sobs Jean assured her host that it was the knife that had been used to murder the woman. He nodded. He himself had found the blade among the bricks of the fireplace.

MARYLAND

Norma Martin's family has been psychic all the way back, usually on the female side. There was a great-grandmother who ran a boardinghouse for the brakemen and motormen who worked on the trolley line to Owings Mills, Maryland. One foggy night a motorman was killed in an accident. Her great-grandmother had forgotten all about the unfortunate fellow when she got off a trolley a year later to walk home. Who would join her but the dead motorman. Since she had befriended him in life she assumed he wanted to protect her on a foggy and rainy night. Every anniversary since she has seen the dead fellow walking with her.

Norma is a young girl living near Baltimore. She likes to spend her summer holidays at her aunt's house in Harford County. Although Norma is aware of her family's background in the occult, she is herself not exactly a believer. At least she wasn't until her cousin complained to her about seeing a ghost. Now Norma had been in her aunt's house before and had not experienced anything, so she questioned her cousin further. Since the other girl was an excellent student and a very logical person, Norma felt that her testimony might be of value. Apparently the cousin had gotten into the habit of staying up very late at night to do her homework. That was in the summer of 1966. In the still of the night she would look up and see a white form go past her toward the bedroom door. Startled, she would turn around but the figure was gone. Not much later she was asleep in the living room when she felt herself awakened by the sound of someone breathing very hard near her. She opened her eyes slightly, and to her bewilderment a strange little man with white hair and a long beard stood next to her bed. A moment later the apparition had vanished. When Norma came back to her aunt's house she wondered about the experience her cousin had reported to her. She was still doubtful and wondered if the whole thing might have been a dream. Shortly after her arrival she woke up in the middle of the night because she had the feeling of a human presence in the room. She looked up and there was the figure of a little man. The sound of his breathing came to her consciousness at the same time. A moment later he had disappeared. It occurred to Norma then that certain spots in her aunt's house had been unusually chilly all along even though it might be very hot outside. Finally convinced that there was something uncanny in her aunt's house, Norma made some inquiries. The little man had been a long-time servant and he had died here, although on the grounds, not in the house directly. Perhaps he had no other place to go than to return to his master's house still trying to serve.

When I was lecturing on extrasensory perception in Baltimore in October of 1968 a pleasant-looking woman came up to me and asked to speak to me quietly. "We have an earthbound restless spirit in our home," she explained and looked around as if she had said something no one else should hear. I assured her that there were thousands of people with similar problems and not to be ashamed of being overheard, especially not in an audience that had come to hear me speak on that very same subject. After the lecture I questioned her further. The Schaefers had moved into their home in Baltimore in November of 1967. They knew that the home was very old but had no idea as to its background or prior tenants. The man who had sold them the house was of very little help except to say there had been many tenants before them. Much later Mrs. Schaefer discovered that no tenant had ever stayed there more than three months and that the list of those who had moved in and out of the house was very long indeed. The owner of the house lived out of town and would not come down to be present at the sale. The Schaefers had never met him, and that too seemed unusual. But at the time they moved in they were excited and happy with their new old home and did not worry about such matters as prior problems, or, heaven forbid, ghosts. As a matter of fact, between November of 1967 and the early spring of 1968 there was nothing in the atmosphere of the house suggesting anything out of the ordinary. One Sunday evening the Schaefers had the visit of a young artist and his wife. In the course of the evening the conversation turned to psychic phenomena and the increased interest the subject seemed to find these days among college people. More as a lark than for serious reasons the young man suggested the use of a Ouija board. He added that he had a feeling there were spirits present in the atmosphere and that they should contact them and find out who they were and why they were present. The Schaefers went along more for amusement's sake than because they felt there was anything haunted about their house. A board was found and immediately the four of them put their hands on it. To their amazement the board came alive instantly. Messages came from it spelled at a rapid pace far more speedily than they could have spelled them even if these messages had originated in their own minds, consciously or unconsciously. What the Ouija kept telling them was that a spirit communicator named David wished to speak to Sara. He identified himself as the son of Elmer and, in a pointed move toward Mrs. Schaefer, kept repeating over and over that he wanted to be her friend. At this point the young artist rose quickly from the board and pointed to one end of the room. His face was pale and sweat pearls appeared on his forehead. Staring toward that end of the room, he said he saw someone standing there and would have no more truck with the Ouija board. Suddenly what had started as light entertainment became heavy with forbidding silence. The Schaefers put the board away with great haste and tried to dismiss the incident with light banter.

Mrs. Schaefer did not really feel that way, for she was aware of the existence of things beyond the pale of the material and had had some interest in research of this kind. She too felt strange at that moment, but thanks to their conversation the young man regained his composure and a moment later was back to his old self. However, so strong had the impact been on him that he refused to discuss the incident then or at any time thereafter. All he would explain to the Schaefers was that something of this kind had happened to him once before and he did not wish to have it happen again. Neither one of the Schaefers had seen anything in the corner of the room to which the young artist had pointed.

After their guests had left the Schaefers went up the

stairs to bed. As she went up Mrs. Schaefer had a strange feeling of a human presence. Before she realized what she was saying she heard herself speak aloud, "You are welcome." There was no fear in her at that time nor ever since, but she had within her the certainty that their home had a spirit resident and that the spirit had made himself known to them through the Ouija board that evening. From that moment on they became increasingly aware of a presence. Their two-year-old grandson would play on the stairs and point at something they couldn't see, describing "the man" standing there. They would hear footsteps crossing the living room, ascending the stairs, and were quite sure that someone was coming up. On one occasion Mr. Schaefer was so sure that a flesh and blood person had invaded their home that he came downstairs with a revolver. The phenomena increased in frequency both in the daytime and at night. Knockings would come from all parts of the house—knockings for which there was no natural explanation. Finally Mrs. Schaefer wondered about the original communicator. Since her given name is Sara she thought that he had tried to contact her, but she knew no David who would fit into a close relationship with her. She decided to search the title of their old home and with some effort found the original land grant which was dated 1836. To her amazement she discovered it had been given to a certain David Patterson. David Patterson had four children, three sons and a daughter. The daughter was named Sara. After her discovery things quieted down. Then they would pick up again. On such occasions she would ask the spirit to please leave and not disturb their house. This would always work for a few days but eventually the noises returned. Mrs. Schaefer then realized that David Patterson was still concerned with his old house and liked to continue living in it.

The Gridiron Club in Baltimore is an up-to-date establishment belying its unusual past. If you look closely you will realize that the house itself is very old and its colonial origins though fixed up are nevertheless still in evidence. There is even a swimming pool now where the old slave quarters used to be. And thereby hangs a ghostly tale. The house goes back about two hundred years and was originally known as the Hillen House. If it weren't for a psychically oriented young lady by the name of Linda Merlo I would never have heard of the Gridiron Club or the Hillen House. Fortunately, for posterity, Miss Merlo lives about a mile away and knows all about it. In the colonial period a Mrs. Hillen owned much of the land around it. In her later years she fell sick and had a nurse in attendance twenty-four hours a day. One day the nurse went out into the hallway for a moment. When she returned her patient was gone. The nurse realized that the slaves might have abducted her patient in order to blackmail her into concessions or freedom, but how could she have disappeared from the room? If there was a secret passage leading down into the slave quarters it was never found. She could not have been kidnapped through the window since the room was on the third floor of the house. The door was impossible too since the nurse had not left the hallway long enough for people to pass through it, and there was no other door to the room. Whichever way the owner of the house was spirited down into the slave quarters, it appears, according to the tradition which may very well be true, that the slaves tried to make her come to terms with them. In the excitement of the moment the sick woman died.

In the course of time the house changed hands often. Eventually it became the property of a family who owned it before it became the Gridiron Club. They were the first ones to realize that something very unusual was going on in their home. The noise of people talking downstairs when no one was about was only one of the phenomena they had to get used to. One of the sons, Ralph, liked to work on motorcycles and cars and frequently went downstairs to wash up. He would walk smack into a party going full blast although he could not understand a single word the voices were saying. As soon as he entered, the noise stopped abruptly. When he left the basement and shut the door behind him he heard the noise resume immediately in what he knew was an empty basement. He would put his working tools carefully away and lock them up. The next day he would find them scattered all over the floor, with some of them missing and never found again. Yet he was sure that no burglar had come into the house. Because of the goings on Ralph took to securely locking all doors and windows. Nevertheless, whenever he did so he would find them wide open the next morning. On one occasion the owner of the house was in the basement locking the windows one by one. As he locked the first window and went on to the second to continue his task he saw the first window open itself again. He locked it again and went on but the phenomenon repeated itself. At that point he said "All right, Mrs. Hillen, I give up," and up he went.

Two of the owner's sons, Ralph and Billy, were sitting in the kitchen when they saw a window open by itself right in front of their very eyes. They jumped to their feet when they heard someone approaching wearing chains dragging behind him. Many slaves were chained at the ankles to prevent them from running away. But it wasn't just the noises that kept reminding the owners of the history of their house. Ralph's fiancée, Barbara, once saw a woman's face in the window and on turning around realized there was no one there who could have caused a reflection. Not much later the figure of a person holding a candle was seen walking down the hall. The owners had the house checked out for any defects whether structural or electrical to account for the many strange noises. That, however, was before the apparition. They realized then that the restless spirit of Mrs. Hillen was still about and that those who had tormented her hadn't found rest either. It is difficult to say whether the patrons of the Gridiron Club are much bothered by these goings on. If they saw the ghost of Mrs. Hillen or of some of the slaves passing by, they might think that the club was putting on a floor show for them. There is no telling what the ghostly slaves think of the swimming pool that now occupies the area where they had to live in those far-off days.

Joseph P. Rosinski is a professional radio announcer in Baltimore, Maryland. He is in his early forties and has had some interest in the occult but not to the point of pursuing it deeply or in great detail. As an avocation Mr. Rosinski has been interested in working with the blind. It was on an autumn night in 1965 that he happened to be reading aloud a textbook to his friend Ed Maff at the Maryland School for the Blind in Overlea which is a suburb of Baltimore. About eight o'clock in the evening the supervisor of the institution came into the classroom where Rosinski and the blind man were sitting, apparently in great agitation. A blind student by the name of Mike Moran was faced with an emergency and had telephoned for help. Apparently the young man had lost his talking book needle. It had rolled somewhere on the rug in his room and he just couldn't find it. Would Mr. Rosinski be kind enough to help out. The radio announcer gladly volunteered to go to Mike Moran's place and read him the text.

That place turned out to be the cupola of an old gingerbread house built in the 1870s located at the corner of the thirteen-hundred block of North Calvert Street in Baltimore. The house seemed unusually quiet on the outside, somewhat neglected, but still showing its once proud exterior, built in a period when houses were far more solid than they are today. There was a proprietor by the name of O'Malley, a white-haired Irishman who spoke with a thick brogue. Somewhat gruffly he pointed toward the stairs to indicate that the blind man lived up there. Rosinski started to walk up. Leaving the dimly lit vestibule he suddenly found himself wondering who he really was. He didn't quite feel like himself at that point. Suddenly he found himself transported back into the gaslit area. Walking up the stairs, he arrived at the top floor and rang the bell to Mike Moran's room. Passing through heavy mahogany doors, he saw that the entire cupola was occupied by one large room. There was an old bedstead with a menacingly high headboard which was about a foot shy of hitting the ceiling. Nearby were a candle stand, an antique marble washstand and other authentic period pieces all done in dark mahogany. Somehow the room seemed frightening to Rosinski. He realized that the room and the furniture had been untouched for years. The room was filled with cigar smoke and an undefinable aroma of the past. However, Rosinski didn't wish to let the strange atmosphere of the room prevent him from doing the job he had come to do. He immediately proceeded to read to the young man the text and then prepared to go home, but the hour was late and it was decided he should spend the night and return in the morning. The bed was large enough to accommodate both of them, so they turned in for the night. Even though Rosinski was very tired from his efforts, he couldn't sleep. As he lay there on the old bed he suddenly felt a female softness under him. In surprise he sat up, thereby awakening Mike Moran also. Rosinski could not see anything but he felt sure there was someone else with them in bed. Mike was blind, yet he immediately "saw" the figure of a young woman on the bed. He was glad Rosinski had come to stay with him, for he was frightened. Rosinski looked toward the head of the bed and what he saw was not very reassuring. There on the bed was the form of a young woman surrounded by an aura of green and blue-gray mist. Somehow he felt that the girl had suffered in the room, and he also had the impression that a baby was connected with the woman in some dramatic way. But the most disturbing feeling of all was *the fact that he no longer felt that he was himself.* He knew for sure now that he was a nineteenth-century doctor visiting a patient in this cupola room. He felt he had to help the poor woman and suffered her agonies with her. Even the way he walked about the room was not his usual gait. It seemed to him that he walked straighter and with a firmer, lighter step than was his usual custom. There was nothing he could do to change this transformation, yet at the same time he was able to observe it clinically and to wonder about it.

After a sleepless night Rosinski returned to his own home. He implored me to go to the house on Calvert Street and do something about the ghostly woman on the bed. I tried to as soon as I was able. I found the house on Calvert Street near Mount Royal without trouble. It is situated just opposite the old Mount Royal Hotel. But I looked in vain for O'Malley. In fact, the house gave every impression of being abandoned or pretty nearly so. The vestibule was dirty and dark. No one opened the door for me and I began to feel I had come too late. Time was of the essence and I did not want to hang around and see whether a living soul might eventually turn up and let me in. Regretfully

I started to walk down the stairs that led from the vestibule to the street outside. Once more I turned and looked back. I had the distinct impression that I was not alone. I could not see anything, but somewhere in the murky dark of the vestibule I felt two outstretched arms. I went back and said in a soft voice, "You are over now and must find peace. Ask for your loved ones to come and get you and take you away from this house where you have found so much unhappiness. There is no need to stay. Everyone you once knew, everyone you once loved, has gone on. You too must go on." I turned and went back to the street. When I looked back once more, the arms were no longer reaching out to me.

NORTH CAROLINA

Since I published my findings regarding the famous Maco Light near Wilmington, North Carolina, people have come to me with new information and others have asked me to shed additional light on the very mysterious light that has puzzled people for many, many years. There are other mysterious lights all over the world, to be sure, such as the Brown Mountain Lights in Tennessee and similar mysterious luminous bodies frequently observed in Washington State. Some of these lights are unquestionably of natural origin and have nothing whatsoever to do with the psychic. Others may be of a parallel nature to the famous Maco Light. I investigated this railroad crossing back in 1964 and published my findings and the testimony of all witnesses I had met in a book called *Ghosts I've Met* in 1965. Under the title "The Case of the Lost Head" I described what had happened to lure me down South to look for an elusive light along a railroad track.

One of the most famous ghosts of the South is railroad conductor Joe Baldwin. The story of Joe and his lantern was known to me, of course, and a few years ago *Life* magazine even dignified it with a photograph of the railroad track near Wilmington, North Carolina, very atmospherically adorned by a greenish lantern, presumably swinging in ghostly hands.

Then one day in early 1964, the legend became reality when a letter arrived from Bill Mitcham, Executive Secretary of the South Eastern North Carolina Beach Association, a public relations office set up by the leading resort hotels in the area centering around Wilmington. Mr. Mitcham proposed that I have a look at the ghost of Joe Baldwin and try to explain once and for all—scientifically—what the famous Maco Light was or is.

In addition, Mr. Mitcham arranged for a lecture on the subject to be held at the end of my investigation and sponsored jointly by the Beach Association and Wilmington College. He promised to roll out the red carpet for Catherine and me, and roll it out he did.

Seldom in the history of ghost hunting has a parapsychologist been received so royally and so fully covered by press, television, and radio, and if the ghost of Joe Baldwin is basking in the reflected glory of all this attention directed toward his personal Ghost Hunter, he is most welcome to it.

If it were not for Joe Baldwin, the bend in the railroad track which is known as Maco Station (a few miles outside of Wilmington) would be a most unattractive and ordinary trestle. By the time I had investigated it and left, in May of 1964, the spot had almost risen to the prominence of a national shrine, and sightseeing groups arrived at all times, especially at night, to look for Joe Baldwin's ghostly light.

Bill Mitcham had seen to it that the world knew about

Joe Baldwin's headless ghost and Hans Holzer seeking same, and no fewer than seventy-eight separate news stories of one kind or another appeared in print during the week we spent in Wilmington.

Before I even started to make plans for the Wilmington expedition, I received a friendly letter from a local student of psychic phenomena, William Edward Cox, Jr., and a manuscript entitled *The Maco Light.* Mr. Cox had spent considerable time observing the strange light, and I quote:

> A favorite "ghost story" in the vicinity of Wilmington, N.C., is that of "Joe Baldwin's Ghost Light," which is alleged to appear at night near Maco, N.C., 12 miles west of Wilmington on the Atlantic Coast Line Railroad.
>
> On June 30–July 1, 1949, this writer spent considerable time investigating the phenomenon. The purpose was to make an accurate check on the behavior of the light under test conditions, with the view toward ascertaining its exact nature.
>
> This light has been observed since shortly after the legend of the Joe Baldwin ghost light "was born in 1867." It is officially reported in a pamphlet entitled "The Story of the Coast Line, 1830–1948." In its general description it resembles a 25-watt electric light slowly moving along the tracks toward the observer, whose best point of observation is on the track itself at the point where the tracks, double at that point, are crossed by a branch of a connecting roadway between U.S. Highway 74–76 and U.S. Highway 19.
>
> The popular explanation is that Conductor Baldwin, decapitated in an accident, is taking the nocturnal walks in search of his head. . . .

After testing the various "natural" theories put forward for the origin of the nocturnal light, Mr. Cox admits:

> Although the general consensus of opinion is that the lights stem from some relatively rare cause, such as the paranormal, "ignis fatuus," etc., the opinions of residents of the Maco vicinity were found by this observer to be more detailed. The

proprietor of the Mobilgas Service Station was noncommittal, and a local customer said he had "never seen the light." A farmer in the area was quite certain that it is caused by automobile headlights, but would not express an opinion upon such lights as were customarily seen there before the advent of the automobile.

The proprietress of the Willet Service Station, Mrs. C. L. Benton, was firmly convinced that it was of "supernatural origin," and that the peculiar visibility of automobile headlights to observers at Maco must be more or less a subsequent coincidence.

She said that her father "often saw it as he loaded the wood burners near there over 60 years ago."

The basic question of the origin and nature of the "Maco Light," or the original light, remains incompletely answered. The findings here reported, due as they are to entirely normal causes, cannot accurately be construed as disproving the existence of a light of paranormal origin at any time in the distant past (or, for that matter, at the present time).

The unquestionable singularity of the phenomenon's being in a locale where it is so easily possible for automobiles to produce an identical phenomenon seems but to relegate it to the enigmatic "realm of forgotten mysteries."

So much for Mr. Cox's painstaking experiment conducted at the site in 1949.

The coming of the Ghost Hunter (and Mrs. Ghost Hunter) was amply heralded in the newspapers of the area. Typical of the veritable avalanche of features was the story in the Charlotte *Observer*:

Can the Spook Hunter De-Ghost Old Joe? The South Eastern N.C. Beach Association invited a leading parapsychologist Saturday to study the ghost of Old Joe Baldwin.

Bill Mitcham, executive director of the association, said he has arranged for Hans Holzer of New York to either prove or disprove the ghostly tales relating to Old Joe.

Holzer will begin his study May 1.

Tales of Joe Baldwin flagging down trains with false signals, waving his lantern on dark summer nights have been repeated since his death in 1867.

Baldwin, a conductor on the Wilmington, Manchester and Augusta Railroad, was riding the rear coach of a train the night of his death. The coach became uncoupled and Baldwin seized a lantern in an effort to signal a passenger train following.

But the engineer failed to see the signal. In the resulting crash, Baldwin was decapitated.

A witness to the wreck later recalled that the signal lantern was flung some distance from the tracks, but that it burned brightly thereafter for some time.

Soon after the accident, there were reports of a mysterious light along the railroad tracks at Maco Station in Brunswick County.

Two lanterns, one green and one red, have been used by trainmen at Maco Station so that engineers would not be confused or deceived by Joe Baldwin's light.

Most helpful in a more serious vein was the Women's Editor of the Wilmington *Star-News,* Theresa Thomas, who had for years taken an interest in the psychic and probably is somewhat sensitive herself. On April 8, 1964, she asked her readers:

Have you ever seen the Maco Light? Have you ever seen Old Joe Baldwin? Or his light, that is? As far as we know, nobody has actually seen Joe himself.

But if you have seen his lantern swinging along the railroad track at Maco, you can be of great help to Hans Holzer, Ghost Hunter, who will be in Wilmington April 29th.

Either write out your experience and send it to us, or call and tell us about it.

Then the feminine point of view crashed the scientific barrier a little as Miss Thomas added:

His [Mr. Holzer's] wife is just as fascinating as he. She is a painter and great-great-great-granddaughter of Catherine the Great of Russia. Mrs. Holzer was born Countess Catherine

Buxhoeveden in a haunted castle in Meran, the Tyrol, in the Italian Alps. And she paints—haven't you guessed?—haunted houses.

My visit was still three weeks away, but the wheels of publicity were already spinning fast and furiously in Wilmington.

Theresa Thomas's appeal for actual witnesses to the ghostly phenomenon brought immediate results. For the first time people of standing took the matter seriously, and those who had seen the light, opened up. Miss Thomas did not disguise her enthusiasm. On April 12 she wrote:

It seems a great many people have seen old Joe Baldwin's light at Maco and most of them are willing—even eager—to talk about it.

Among the first to call was Mrs. Larry Moore, 211 Orange Street, who said she had seen the light three or four times at different seasons of the year.

The first time it was a cloudy, misty winter night and again in the summer, misty again. Her description of the light was "like a bluish yellow flame." She and her companions walked down the track and the light came closer as they approached the trestle. When they reached the center of the trestle with the light apparently about 10 feet away, it disappeared.

Mrs. Thelma Daughty, 6 Shearwater Drive, Wrightsville Beach, says she saw it on a misty spring night. It was about 7 or 8 o'clock in the evening and the reddish light appeared to swing along at about knee height.

Mrs. Margaret Jackson, 172 Colonial Circle, a native of Vienna, Austria, saw it about seven years ago on a hazy night, a "glary shine" steady and far away but always the same distance ahead of them.

Dixie Rambeau, 220 Pfeiffer Avenue, saw it about 1 a.m. Friday morning. She says it was "real dark" and the light appeared as a red pinpoint at a distance up the track, as it neared it became yellowish white, then closer still it was a mixed red and white.

She recalls that she and her companions watched it come closer to the left side of the track and that as it came close the reflection on the rail almost reached them. At about 10 feet away it reversed its process and as they walked toward it, it disappeared. Once it appeared to cross over. They watched it five or six times, she said.

Mrs. Marvin Clark, 406 Grace Street, a practical nurse, states that she and her husband saw the light 15 years ago. It was about midnight on a cloudy, rainy night. They were standing in the middle of the tracks and "it looked like a light on a train coming at full speed."

Mrs. Clark described the light as "the color of a train light."

"We picked up our little girl and ran. All of us have always seen reflections of automobiles but beyond a doubt it was the Maco Light."

Mrs. Lase V. Dail of Carolina Beach also has a story to tell. It seems she and her husband came home late one night from Fayetteville.

She writes: "As we left the cut off and headed into 74-76 Highway, I shall never forget the experience we had . . ." She goes on, "All at once a bright light came down the road towards us, first I figured it was a car. But decided if so it had only one light. On it came steadily toward us.

"Then I figured it was a train, yet I heard nothing, and as suddenly as it appeared it vanished. I can say it was quite a weird feeling. I have often thought of it. I have heard many versions, but never one like this."

Three days later, Miss Thomas devoted still another full column to people who had witnessed the ghost light.

Mrs. Marjorie H. Rizer of Sneads Ferry writes: "I have seen the light three times. The last and most significant time was about a year and a half ago. My husband, three young sons and a companion from the United States Naval Hospital at Camp Lejeune were with me and we saw the same thing. It was about 10:30 p.m. and we were returning from a ball game. We decided to go to Maco since we were so near and the young man with us didn't believe there was anything to our story.

"The sky was cloudy and a light mist was falling. We parked the car beside the track and sure enough, there was the light down the track. I stayed in the car with my sons, and my husband and the corpsman walked down the track toward the light.

"The light would alternately dim and then become very bright. The two men walked perhaps a quarter of a mile down the track before they returned. They said the light stayed ahead of them, but my sons and I saw the light beween them and us.

"It looked as if the light would come almost to where we were parked and then it would wobble off down the track and disappear. In a moment it would reappear and do the same time after time.

"When we had been there for about an hour and started to leave, a train approached going toward Wilmington. The light was a short distance away from us. As the train passed the light, it rose and hovered over the train. We could clearly see the top of the train as the light became very bright.

"It stayed over the train until it had passed then disappeared back down the track and finally it looked as if someone had thrown it off into the woods.

"As we pulled away from the track the light came back on the track and weaved backward and forward down the track as it had been doing."

And still the letters poured in. On April 22, after half a column devoted to my imminent arrival in the area, Miss Thomas printed a letter from a young man who had taken some interesting pictures:

He is J. Everett Huggins, home address 412 Market Street, Wilmington. The letter is addressed to Bill Mitcham and reads in part: "I read with interest the articles on your 'ghost survey,' especially since I saw the Maco light less than two weeks ago and was actually able to catch Old Joe on film.

"On the nights of April 1 and 2 a schoolmate of mine and I went to Maco Station in the hopes of seeing the light. We saw nothing on Friday, April 1, but we had more success on Saturday, when it was a little darker. Around 10:30 we saw a yellow light about 100 yards down the track from us (this distance is only a guess). It seemed to be about 10 feet above the tracks and looked as if it were moving slowly toward us for a while, then it went back and died out.

"The light appeared maybe three times in succession for periods up to what I would estimate to be about thirty seconds.

"I attempted to take two time exposures with my camera. Unfortunately I did not have a tripod, and so I had to hold the camera in my hands, which made clear results impossible. The pictures are not spectacular—just a small spot on each of the color transparencies—but they are pictures. If you are interested I will have some copies made.

"My friends had kidded me about the light, so I noted some details to try to end their skepticism. The headlights of cars traveling west on Highway 74 could be seen in the distance, and no doubt many who think they see Old Joe only see these lights. Old Joe could be distinguished in several ways, however. First, the light had a yellower tone than did the auto headlights.

"Secondly, unlike the headlights which grow brighter and brighter and then suddenly disappear, the Maco light would gradually grow brighter and then gradually fade out. Thirdly, the Maco light produced a reflection on the rails that was not characteristic of the headlights.

"More interesting was the fact that the reflection on the rails was seen only on a relatively short stretch of track. By observing the reflection, we could tell that the light moved backward and forward on the rails. It always remained directly above the tracks.

"I had seen the light once before, in 1956. It was on a cold winter night, and the light was brighter."

As the day of our arrival grew nearer, the tempo of the press became more hectic. On April 26, Arnold Kirk wrote in the Wilmington *Star-News:*

This tiny Brunswick County village, nestled in a small clearing a few miles west of Wilmington off U.S. Highway 74, is rapidly gaining acclaim as the "Ghost Capital" of North Carolina.

Its few dozen inhabitants, mostly farmers of moderate means, have suddenly found their once-peaceful nights disturbed by scores of vehicles sparring for vantage points from which to view the famous "Maco Light."

While the legend of the light and Old Joe Baldwin, the "Ghost" of Maco, has long been known, its popularity has become intense only in recent months.

Elaborate plans have already been made to welcome Holzer to the Port City. The mayors of all the towns in New Hanover and Brunswick counties, in addition to county commissioners from both counties, have agreed to be at New Hanover County Airport Wednesday at 7:43 p.m. when the "ghost hunter's" plane arrives.

Also on hand to greet the noted parapsychologist will be 1,000 high-school students, carrying, appropriately enough, lighted lanterns! The lanterns were purchased by the city years ago to offer warmth to trees and plants during blustery winter months.

Adding to the fanfare of the event will be the first public offering of "The Ballad of Old Joe Baldwin," written by the senior English class of New Hanover High School.

The reception was a bash that would have made Old Joe Baldwin feel honored. A little later, we tried to sneak out to Maco and have a first glance at the haunted spot. The results were disappointing.

It was not so much that the ghost did not show, but what did show up was most disturbing. The Wilmington *Star-News* summed it up like this:

An unwilling Old Joe Baldwin exercised his ghostly prerogative Wednesday night by refusing to perform before what may have been his largest audience.

Huddled in small clusters along the railroad tracks near the center of this tiny Brunswick County village, an estimated 250 persons stared into the gloomy darkness in hopes of catching a glimpse of the famous "Maco Light."

But the light would not offer the slightest flicker.

Holzer's announced visit to the scene of Baldwin's ghastly demise gave no comfort to the few dozen residents of Maco. By

10 o'clock, dozens of cars lined both sides of the narrow Maco road and scores of thrill-seeking teenagers had spilled onto the railroad track.

If Joe Baldwin had decided to make an appearance, his performance no doubt would have been engulfed in the dozens of flashlights and battery-powered lanterns searching through the darkness for at least a mile down the track.

Several times, the flashlights and lanterns were mistaken for the "Maco Light," giving hope that the mysterious glow would soon appear.

A large portion of the track was illuminated by the headlights of a jeep and small foreign car scurrying back and forth along both sides of the track. A young girl created an anxious moment when she mistook a firefly for the "Maco Light" and released a penetrating scream that sliced through the pitch-darkness.

Holzer's visit to Maco on Wednesday night was mostly for the benefit of photographers and reporters who met the noted parapsychologist at the New Hanover County airport earlier that night.

His second visit to the crossing will be kept a closely guarded secret in hopes the "ghost hunter" will be able to conduct his investigation of the light without being interrupted by pranksters and playful teenagers.

Soon I realized that it would be impossible for us to go out to the tracks alone. Crowds followed us around and crowds were ever present at the spot, giving rise to a suspicion in my mind that these people were not in a working mood while we were visiting their area. Evidently we were the most exciting thing that had happened to them for some time.

Finally, the day of a scheduled press conference arrived, and at ten o'clock in the morning, before a battery of klieg lights and microphones set up at the magnificent Blockade Runner Hotel on the beach, I started to talk in person to those who had come to tell me about their encounters with Joe Baldwin's ghost.

In addition to those who had written to Miss Thomas

and reaffirmed their original stories, others came forward who had not done so previously. There was William McGirt, an insurance executive, who called the light "buoyant," flicking itself on and off, as it were, and fully reflected on the iron rails. But you cannot see it looking east, he told me, only when you look toward Maco Station.

Margaret Bremer added to her previously told story by saying the light looked to her "like a kerosene lantern swaying back and forth."

Her husband, Mr. Bremer, had not planned on saying anything but I coaxed him. He admitted finally that twelve years ago, when his car was standing straddled across the tracks, he had seen a light coming toward him. It flickered like a lamp, and when it came closer it flared up. As an afterthought he added, "Something strange—suddenly there seemed to be a rush of air, as if a train were coming from Wilmington."

"Was there?" I inquired cautiously.

"No, of course not. We wouldn't have had the car across the track if a train were expected."

Mrs. Laura Collins stepped forward and told me of the time she was at the trestle with a boy who did not believe in ghosts, not even Joe Baldwin's. When the light appeared, he sneered at it and tried to explain it as a reflection. Six feet away from the boy, the light suddenly disappeared and reappeared in back of him—as if to show him up! Mrs. Collins, along with others, observed that misty weather made the light appear clearer.

Next in the parade of witnesses came Mrs. Elizabeth Finch of Wilmington, who had offered her original testimony only the day before.

"It appeared to me many times," she said of the light; "looked like a lantern to me. Two years ago, we were parked across the tracks in our car—we were watching for a train of course, too—when I saw two dazzling lights from both sides. It was a winter evening, but I suddenly felt very hot. There was a red streak in front of the car, *and then I saw what was a dim outline of a man walking with a lantern and swinging it.* Mind you, it was a bare outline," Mrs. Finch added in emphasis, "and it did have a head . . . just kept going, then suddenly he disappeared inside the tracks."

"Did you ever have psychic experiences before, Mrs. Finch?" I wanted to know.

"Yes, when we lived in a house in Masonborough, I used to hear noises, steps, even voices out of nowhere—later, I was told it was haunted."

I thanked Mrs. Finch, wondering if the local legend had impressed her unconscious to the point where she did see what everyone had said was there—or whether she really saw the outline of a man.

I really have no reason to doubt her story. She struck me as a calm, intelligent person who would not easily make up a story just to be sensational. No, I decided, Mrs. Finch might very well have been one of the very few who saw more than just the light.

"I tell you why it can't be anything ordinary," Mr. Trussle, my next informant, said. "Seven years ago, when I saw the light on a damp night about a mile away from where I was standing, I noticed its very rapid approach. It disappeared fast, went back and forth as if to attract attention to something. *It was three foot above the track about the height of where a man's arm might be.*

"At first, it seemed yellowish white; when I came closer, it looked like kind of pinkish. Now an ordinary car headlight wouldn't go back and forth like that, would it?"

I agreed it was most unlikely for an automobile headlight to behave in such an unusual manner.

Mrs. Miriam Moore saw it three times, always on misty, humid nights. "I had a funny ringing in my ears when I reached the spot," she said. She was sure what she saw was a lamp swinging in a slow motion. Suddenly, she broke into a cold sweat for no reason at all. I established that she was a psychic person and had on occasion foretold the deaths of various members of her family.

E. S. Skipper is a dapper little man in the golden years of life, but peppery and very much alert. He used to be a freight skipper on the Atlantic Coast Line and grew up with the Maco Light the way Niagara kids grow up with the sight of the Falls.

"I've seen it hundreds of times," he volunteered. "I've seen it flag trains down—it moved just like a railroad lantern would. On one occasion I took my shot gun and walked toward it. As I got nearer, the light became so bright I could hardly look. Suddenly, it disappeared into the old Catholic cemetery on the right side of the tracks."

"Cemetery?" I asked, for I had not heard of a cemetery in this area.

Mr. Skipper was quite certain that there was one. I promised to look into this immediately. "Since you came so close to the light, Mr. Skipper," I said, "perhaps you can tell me what it looked like close up."

"Oh, I got even closer than that—back in 1929. I remember it well. It was two o'clock in the morning. I got to within six foot of it."

"What did you see?"

"I saw a flame. I mean, in the middle of the light, there was, unmistakably, a flame burning."

"Like a lantern?"

"Like a lantern."

I thanked Mr. Skipper and was ready to turn to my last witness, none other than Editor Thomas herself, when Mrs.

E. R. Rich, who had already given her account in the newspaper, asked for another minute, which I gladly gave her.

"Ten years ago," Mrs. Rich said, "we were at the track one evening. My son Robert was in the car with me, and my older son went down the track to watch for the light. Suddenly not one but two lights appeared at the car. They were round and seemed to radiate and to sparkle—for a moment they hung around, then one left, the other stayed. My feet went ice cold at this moment and I felt very strange."

"Miss Thomas," I said, "will you add your own experiences to this plethora of information?"

"Gladly," the Women's Editor of the *Star-News* replied. "There were three of us, all newspaper women, who decided a few weeks ago to go down to the trestle and not see anything."

"I beg your pardon?"

"We'd made up our minds not to be influenced by all the publicity Joe Baldwin's ghost was getting."

"What happened?"

"When we got to the track, dogs were baying as if disturbed by something in the atmosphere. We parked on the dirt road that runs parallel to the track and waited. After a while, the light appeared. It had a yellow glow. Then, suddenly, there were two lights, one larger than the other, swaying in the night sky.

"The lights turned reddish after a while. There was no correlation with car lights at all. I thought at first it was a train bearing down on us, that's how big the lights appeared. Just as suddenly the lights disappeared. One light described an arc to the left of the track, landing in the grass."

"Just as those old tales say Joe's lantern did, eh?"

"It seems so, although it is hard to believe."

"What else did you notice?"

"I had the feeling I was not alone."

And there you have it. Mass hysteria? Self-hypnosis? Suggestion? Could all these people make up similar stories?

Although the Maco Light is unique in its specific aspects, there are other lights that have been observed at spots where tragedies have occurred. There are reports of apparitions in Colorado taking the form of concentrated energy, or light globes. I don't doubt that the human personality is a form of energy that cannot be destroyed, only transmuted. The man who heard the sound of a train, the psychic chill several people experienced, the flame within the light, the two lights clearly distinguished by the newspaper women—possibly Joe's lantern and the headlight of the onrushing train—all these add up to a case.

That evening, at Bogden Hall, before an audience of some five hundred people of all ages, I stated my conviction that the track at Maco Station was, indeed, haunted. I explained that the shock of sudden death might have caused Joe Baldwin's etheric self to become glued to the spot of the tragedy, re-enacting the final moments over and over again.

I don't think we are dealing here with an "etheric impression" registered in the atmosphere and not possessing a life of its own. The phantom reacts differently with various people and seems to me a true ghost, capable of attempting communication with the living, but not fully aware of his own status or of the futility of his efforts.

I was, and am, convinced of the veracity of the phenomenon and, by comparing it to other "weaving lights" in other areas, can only conclude that the basic folklore is on the right track, except that Joe isn't likely to be looking for his head—he is rather trying to keep an imaginary train from running into his uncoupled car, which of course exists now only in his thought world.

And until someone tells Joe all's well on the line now,

he will continue to wave his light. I tried to say the right words for such occasions, but I was somewhat hampered by the fact that I did not have Mrs. Ethel Meyers, my favorite medium, with me; then, too, the Wilmington people did not like the idea of having their town ghost go to his reward and leave the trestle just another second-rate railroad track.

The folks living alongside it, though, wouldn't have minded one bit. They can do without Joe Baldwin and his somewhat motley admirers.

Suddenly the thought struck me that we had no proof that a Joe Baldwin had ever really existed in this area. The next morning I went to the Wilmington Public Library and started to dig into the files and historical sources dealing with the area a hundred years ago. Bill Mitcham and I started to read all the newspapers from 1866 onward, but after a while we gave up. Instead, I had a hunch which, eventually, paid off. If Joe Baldwin was physically fit to work on the railroad in so hazardous a job as that of a train man, he must have been well enough to be in the Armed Forces at one time or another.

I started to search the Regimental Records from 1867 on backward. Finally I found in volume V, page 602, of a work called North Carolina Regiments, published in 1901, the following entry:

"Joseph Baldwin, Company F, 26th N. C. T., badly wounded in the thigh. Battle of Gettysburg. July 1, 1863."

It was the only Joseph Baldwin listed in the area, or, for that matter, the state.

I also inquired about the old Catholic cemetery. It was, indeed, near the railroad track, but had been out of use for many years. Only oldsters still remembered its existence. Baldwin may have been Catholic, as are many residents of the area. Time did not permit me to look among the dilapidated tombstones for a grave bearing the name of Joe Baldwin.

But it would be interesting to find it and see if all of Joe Baldwin lies buried in sacred ground!

On November 17, 1964, the Wilmington *Morning Star* in their Letter to the Editor column published a communication from one Curtis Matthews in which Mr. Matthews stated he knew all about the Maco Light and what it really was. He assured the readers of the Wilmington *Morning Star* that, when he was going to New Hanover High School back in 1928 through 1933, they would make a sport out of fooling their dates so they would be real scared and cling to their arms. This was accomplished by getting out of the car and walking along the tracks and watching the mysterious Maco Light come toward them. "The light would startle you as it came down the tracks and the reflection off the tracks made it more eerie. Afterward we checked on it and determined it to be cars coming toward Wilmington at that point and encountering hills before passing Maco itself. This caused the lights to flicker off and come back on again. We thought the reflection of the lights off the tracks made it look as scary as it did. If no automobiles came by some of the fellows went up ahead and waved lights or lanterns. No one was disappointed then. We never told our dates of our findings. It would have ruined everything." Mr. Matthews, of course, makes it all sound just too easy. He was, of course, unaware of the extensive work done along these lines by Mr. Cox and other scientists with or without dates clinging to their arms.

I had thought no more about Wilmington and the Maco Light when a communication reached me on October 28, 1968. An alert young man by the name of Mack Etheridge, then age fifteen, wanted me to hear of his experiences with the Maco Light. He had been interested in the occult for many years prior to his contacting me but had never had any actual psychic experiences even though other members of his family had. Mack's family, including himself, was traveling from Maryland to South Carolina to visit his grandmother that summer. They decided to route their trip through Wilmington to have a look at the fabled Maco Light.

The family arrived in Wilmington on August 7, 1968, around 2:30 in the morning. They didn't intend to stay but only ride through. They had difficulty finding the bend in the railroad track where the Maco trestle is located, due to the darkness and the lack of signs. Nevertheless, disregarding the late hour, they continued to look for it. They knocked on doors, but no one answered. Finally they were riding back toward Wilmington on Route 74-76 when they noticed a new road parallel to it under construction. They decided to stop at a dimly lit trailer as a last try to obtain some information. A young woman directed them back down the highway from where they had just come and told them how to continue toward the track. There was a dirt road parallel to it which they assumed was the road to take. With their eyes wide open and directed toward the track, they followed the dirt road slowly till it came to a small house and ended. They realized they had gone down the wrong road. Retracing their steps they suddenly noticed a small sign reading *Maco, two miles.* They followed the sign and exactly two miles later arrived at the proper spot. The moment they arrived Mr. Etheridge, Sr., parked the car across the track and shut off the lights, and the family stayed in the car quietly and expectantly, hopefully awaiting some sort of glimpse of the light.

It was an exceptionally clear night with a full moon. Nevertheless, a moment later Mr. Etheridge, Sr., noticed a very bright light and pointed it out to his family. The light was not moving up the track toward them. At first it did not appear to be very bright and Mack immediately dismissed it as being a train and not the Maco Light because it seemed to him to be far too bright. But several minutes later the light approached and remained constant. Mack was no longer sure that the light belonged to an approaching train since there was absolutely no sound. Now the light would alternately dim and become bright again. He could observe it with the naked eye and noted that it was a yellowish light one foot in diameter and extremely bright. It would flare up to its brightest intensity for two seconds and then slowly fade out. Sometimes when it faded out it would appear to be farther up the track. There were times when the light would pulsate and he also noticed that there was a hazy luminosity around it when it faded out. At its closest point the light seemed about two hundred feet away. He noticed with mounting excitement that when it was very close the light would slowly swing at knee level as a lantern would in the hands of a man. When the light was closest it appeared to him that it shone on a relatively short stretch of track.

At this point Mr. Etheridge, Sr., reminded his family that they had brought binoculars, and immediately they put them to good use observing the phenomenon for several minutes through them. The binoculars had a seven by thirty-five power and were in excellent condition. "The following," Mack Etheridge explained, "was seen wholly by me and will be totally new to you and to your writings."

As he was gazing at the light through the binoculars about a quarter mile up the track it faded out again and he quite naturally expected it to reappear as the same, but instead it reappeared accompanied by two other lights. These additional lights appeared instantly to the side of the track. There was a red light to the far left; a few feet to the right of that was a small green light, and several feet to the right of that was the usual yellow light, the largest of them. Mack could clearly see the center green light float into the red one and become part of it, which was then all red. Then the red moved into the yellow by way of a yellow cord. This connecting link first appeared in the yellow light, then shot forward to the red one connecting the two. Gradually it drew the red light into itself to form the usual bright light observed as the Maco Light.

Mack was amazed at what he had just seen. He followed the light as it moved up the track to perform various maneuvers, only to move back down to repeat the previous procedure. He saw it happen twice and described what he observed to his family. They, however, could only see two of the lights due to the distance and faintness. But as seen through the binoculars the single light seemed to rise up in the air above the track, possibly to the height of a telephone pole. After the three lights had formed Mack also noticed the colors visible together a few times. At this point a train was approaching from the opposite direction and it became necessary to move the car off the track. When the train went by, the light faded out, only to return after the train had passed. At that time of night Highway 74 and 76, the crucial point in the observation of the Maco Light, was virtually desolate. They had passed only a few cars in the hours they spent searching for the station. I had surmised that the lights represented Joe Baldwin's lantern and the headlights of an onrushing train, but Mack Etheridge took issue with that explanation. He assured me that in his estimation no train could have been in sight of the track a quarter of a mile away. The two lights to him were completely separate, and as one would fade out another would continue its strange behavior.

Assuming that the Etheridges were sober and sane people, and their observation correct, it would bear out some of the previous testimony reported by me. What is fascinating in this additional report is the fact that some sort of human agency seems behind the movements of the lights.

This was by no means the end of Joe Baldwin and his lost head. In 1970 I received another communication from a certain Daniel Harrington of Flushing, Long Island. Mr. Harrington had visited the Maco Light, inspired by my account of it. He had brought along a camera, since he was somewhat of a camera fan, in the hopes of capturing the elusive light on film. His black and white pictures were taken with time exposure, 5 or 6 seconds, but unfortunately without tripods. Thus the results would, of necessity, be somewhat blurred. He had clearly seen a large light on the track circling, bobbing and weaving about. In one of the two photographs submitted to me the light seems extremely large in relation to the track. That, however, as Mr. Harrington pointed out, is due to the angle of the camera. In the first photograph there is a single light. In the second shot there are clearly three separate lights: round, brightly lit orbs of luminosity—two large ones and a small one. Mr. Harrington assured me there were no cars passing by when these pictures were taken.

So it would appear that today, seven years after my original visit to the spot, Joe Baldwin is still merrily walking along the track and holding up the lantern to stop an imaginary train. No one has yet come up with a better explanation.

OKLAHOMA

I am indebted to a young lady by the name of Lori Buzza for the verified account of a friend who has been psychic from her early years onward. The girl's name is Penny McDaniel. Today she has come to terms with her ESP faculty and is no longer frightened by it. She is able to foretell when a telephone might ring and has, on occasion, done trance work in which personalities of the deceased have come through her. But in 1965 when she was in her early teens something happened that really frightened her, when she visited her grandmother in an area of Oklahoma that was Indian territory until fairly recently. Part of the present-day house is built over a spot where there was once an old log cabin. One of the rooms of the house is in fact built on the exact foundations of that nonexistent cabin.

There were other guests besides her parents and Penny, so the question of where each was to sleep came up and caused some problems. The grandmother tried to fix the young girl a cot in the living room, but Penny insisted that that was perfectly ridiculous since there seemed to be a very nice bedroom not being used by anyone. After an embarrassing silence her grandmother explained that the bedroom Penny was referring to would not be available to her either. Why not, Penny wanted to know. Because, explained her grandmother, somewhat uneasily, people had been hearing strange noises and seeing inexplicable things in that room and it had been finally closed off and no one had entered it for years. Nonsense, Penny decided. She was not afraid of such things as haunted rooms. There was no such thing as ghosts and if the others were too scared to sleep in the closed-off room, she certainly wasn't. Finally her grandmother shrugged and gave her the key to the room. No one wanted to come along with her to help her make up the bed so Penny went on her own. When she stuck the key into the lock and opened the door she was greeted by musty air. Evidently the room had not been aired out or entered for many years. Everything was covered with thick dust, but the hour was late and Penny was not in the mood to clean up. All she did was make up the bed and go to sleep, not touching anything else.

It must have been the middle of the night when she awoke with a jolt. She had a feeling of a presence in the room. She looked around and at the foot of her bed stood a woman dressed in pioneer clothes. Her figure was completely white and as Penny looked at her she seemed to fade away slowly. Penny decided she was dreaming and started to turn over and go back to sleep. A moment later when she was still not fully asleep she heard sounds by the side of her bed. It sounded as if some animal were passing by. She turned and to her horror saw the perfect imprints of a dog's forepaws on the side of the bed. At this point she screamed. Her mother came rushing in and turned on the lights. At the side of the bed there were paw prints in the dust on the floor and not far away from the paw prints, at the front of the bed, were a set of woman's footprints.

After this Penny did not sleep for the rest of the night. She sat up in the living room waiting for daybreak. Her mother had in the meantime gone back to sleep, assuming that Penny would be all right away from the haunted room. It was around six o'clock in the morning when Penny had a strong impulse to get up and walk out of the house. As if driven by an unseen force she found herself walking in the yard, turning around the back of the house and directing her steps to a spot directly under the windows of the very bedroom she had slept in earlier that night. As she looked down on the ground she discovered the skeleton of a hand and a foot and scraps of scalp placed there in a perfect triangle. Looking at what she instantly knew were human remains, she screamed for her mother and then passed out. It was not until three days later that she came to in a local hospital. As soon as she had recovered her wits Penny, her brother Tom, and Mrs. McDaniel, the mother, joined forces to investigate the occurrence. Digging into local historical records, they discovered that there had been ample reason for the frightening event to take place.

Back during pioneer days a log cabin had stood on the spot where the haunted room was later built. In it lived a family consisting of a husband, wife, and a sheepdog. There were no neighbors directly nearby so no one is sure exactly when the tragedy happened. One day the nearest neighbors, some distance away, saw smoke rising from the homestead and decided to investigate. On approaching the house they discovered that the cabin had been burned by Indians and all the family killed including the dog. The bodies were all burned except the woman's. It was already late in the day and the neighbors decided not to brave the Indians they assumed were still lurking around the area and returned to their own homes. The next morning they returned to bury the family. It was then that they discovered that the Indians had apparently returned during the night and had cut off the woman's right hand and foot and had also scalped her. As they were searching through the rubble of the cabin they discovered the missing hand and foot and scalp placed in a triangle beneath where two windows of the log cabin had been in back of the house. They had been placed there in some sort of ritual to appease the gods of the Indians.

SOUTH CAROLINA

Susan D. of Columbia, South Carolina, was born in Texas and is presently twenty-eight years old. Her father was in the service at first and after the war her parents moved to South Carolina, where her father's family had lived for generations. Susan is the eldest of three sisters. They grew up in a small town in the upper section of the state and then moved to Columbia, where her father became the superintendent of a state boarding school for unusual students. At that point Susan was seventeen. Later she entered a local college and stayed for two years. She is presently living with her husband, who is also in education, and they have a little boy. Because of a background of premonitions she had some interest in studying psychic phenomena, but this interest was rather on the vague side.

The first complete incident Susan can remember happened when she was just twelve years old. At that time she had spent the night with her grandmother, also named Susan. During the night the little girl dreamed her grandmother had died. She was awakened from her dream by her cousin Kenneth with the sad news that her grandmother had indeed died during the night.

There had always been a close relationship between her and her father, so when her father was taken to the hospital with a heart attack in 1967 she was naturally concerned. After a while the doctors allowed him to return to his home life, and by the time her little boy was a year old in March of 1968 her father seemed completely well and there was no thought of further illness on the family's mind. Two days after they had all been together for the first birthday celebration of her little boy she awoke in the middle of the night with an overpowering anxiety about her father's well-being. She became convinced that her father would leave them soon. The next morning she telephoned her sister and started to discuss her concern for her father. At that moment her father interrupted her call by asking her sister to get her mother immediately. He died on the way to the hospital that very afternoon.

Susan's father had had a very close friend by the name of Joe F. with whom he had shared a great love of college football games. Joe F. had passed on a short time before. A little later, Susan and her husband attended one of the games of the University of South Carolina. This was in the fall of 1968. On the way to their seats Susan looked up toward the rear section of the arena and quickly turned her head back to her husband. She was so upset at what she saw that it took her a moment to calm down and take her seat. There, not more than eight feet away from her, stood her late father just as he had looked in life. Moreover, she heard him speak to her clearly and in his usual tone of voice. Her husband had not noticed anything. She decided not to tell him about it. As she slowly turned her head back to where they had come from she noticed her father again. This time Joe F., his life-long friend, was with him. The two dead men were walking down the walkway in front of the seats and she had a good opportunity to see them clearly. They seemed as much alive then as they had ever been when she knew them both in the flesh.

Susan D. has an aunt by the name of Mrs. Fred V. They had frequently discussed the possibility of life after death and psychic phenomena in general, especially after the death of the aunt's husband, which had come rather unexpectedly. It was then that the two women realized that they had shared a similar extraordinary experience. Mrs. Fred V. had also gone to a football game at the University of South Carolina, but her visit was a week later, for a different game than Susan's had been. Since the two women had not met for some time there had been no opportunity to discuss Susan's original psychic experience at the football game with her aunt. Nevertheless, Mrs. V. told her niece that something quite extraordinary had happened to her at that particular football game. She too had seen the two dead men watch the game as if they were still very much in the flesh. To Mrs. V. this was a signal that her own husband was to join them, for the three had been very good and close friends in life. As it happened she was right. He passed on soon afterwards.

Susan D. has heard the voice of her father since then on several occasions, although she hasn't seen him again. It appears that her father intercedes frequently when Susan is about to lose her temper in some matter or take a wrong step. On such occasions she hears his voice telling her to take it easy.

One of the best known ghosts of South Carolina's low country is the so-called Gray Man of Pawley's Island. A number of local people claim they have seen him gazing seaward from the dunes, especially when a hurricane is about to break. He is supposed to warn of impending disaster. Who the Gray Man of Pawley's Island is is open to question. According to *A Perceptive Survey of South Carolina Ghosts* by Worth Gatewood, published in 1962, he may be the original Percival Pawley who so loved his island that he felt impelled to watch over it even after he passed on. But Mr. Gatewood gives more credence to a beautiful and romantic account of the origin of the specter. According to this story a young man who was to be married to a local belle left for New York to attend to some business but on his way back was shipwrecked and lost at sea. After a year's time the young woman married his best friend and settled down on Pawley's Island with her new husband. Years later the original young man returned, again shipwrecked and rescued by one of his former fiancée's servants.

When he realized that his love had married in the meantime, he drowned himself at the nearby shore. All this happened, if we believe it happened, a long time ago, because the Gray Man has been seen ever since 1822, or perhaps even earlier than that. A Mrs. Eileen Weaver, according to Mr. Gatewood's account, saw the specter on her veranda and it was indeed a dim outline of a man in gray. There had been unexplained footsteps on her veranda and doors opening and closing by themselves, untouched by human hands.

A businessman by the name of William Collins who did not believe in ghosts, not even in South Carolina ghosts, found himself on the lookout to check on the rising surf on the morning of famed Hurricane Hazel. As he was walking down the dunes he noticed the figure of a man standing on the beach looking seaward. Collins challenged him, thinking that perhaps he was a neighbor who had come out to check on the rising tide, but the stranger paid no attention. Busy with his task, Collins forgot about this and by the time he looked up the stranger had gone. According to the weather forecast, however, the hurricane had shifted directions and was not likely to hit the area, so Collins and his family went to bed that night, sure that the worst was over. At five o'clock in the morning he was aroused from bed by heavy pounding on his door. Opening it, he could feel the house shake from the wind rising to tremendous force. On his veranda stood a stranger wearing a gray fishing cap and a common work shirt and pants, all of it in gray. He told Collins to get off the beach since the storm was coming in. Collins thanked him and ran upstairs to wake his family. After the excitement of the storm had passed Collins wondered about the man who had warned him to get off the island. Intelligently he investigated the matter, only to find that no one had seen the man, nor had any of his neighbors had a guest fitting his description. The state highway patrolman on duty also had not seen anyone come or go, and there is only one access road, the causeway over the marshes.

TEXAS

When Texas joined the union it had the option of becoming five separate states or remaining one large state. As we all know the new state chose to be one state. If it is larger than states are supposed to be in a federal union it also has a tendency to aim for bigger and better things. Not necessarily to accomplish them, but to try to interest other states and people in them. So it doesn't come as a great surprise that there are comparatively more psychic occurrences in Texas than there are in a smaller state. Also, its colorful history, during which the area changed hands several times, has contributed to the number of psychic incidents from the past. Texas contains at least two major population centers, Dallas and Houston. Thus the psychic occurrences in Texas differ greatly in nature from hauntings in, let us say, the Carolinas or Virginia. In the latter they are frequently connected with homesteads and very old houses. In Texas the phenomena take on a more personal note and seem to be tied in with people rather than locations.

Elaine M. is a pleasent woman in her thirties living about 50 miles from Houston. On my last visit to that city I talked to her about two of the many strange experiences she has had. These two shook her up more than anything else that had happened to her and I began to see why.

The first event happened in the fall of 1957. Elaine and her husband had just received word that their two closest friends, Jack and Linda S., with one of their children, had died of asphyxiation in their home in Florida. Apparently Linda had been slated for brain surgery two weeks later and had not been able to face it. The death by gas of three people so close to her depressed Elaine very much. She and Linda had been very close, cared for each other and worried about each other's children. But after several months she began to come out of her depression. In January of 1958 Texas underwent an unusually hard cold spell. It was therefore necessary to use additional heaters, and it was the custom in Mr. and Mrs. M.'s home to leave the gas heat on all night. In the kitchen there was ordinary open gas stove, but they kept the flame low, and since the windows were all locked there didn't seem to be any danger of any of the flames going out and causing gas to leak into the apartment.

One night, at two o'clock in the morning, Elaine felt herself waking up. Clearly as if she were standing next to her she heard her good friend Linda speak to her. "Elaine," the voice said, "get up and see about the boys." Elaine was terrified and fully awake now. As she was about to jump out of bed she smelled gas. She ran to the boys' room and found the gas jets wide open. In another five or ten minutes the gas would have caused an explosion from the other heaters. Quickly Elaine turned them off. At this moment she felt a cool moist cloud surround her and clearly heard her late friend Linda laugh and say, "I told you." For several days after this Elaine was upset over what had occurred. She was grateful to her late friend for having warned her but at the same time she did not easily accept the communication from the beyond. A few days had passed when she found herself discussing the entire matter on the telephone with a minister. Somehow the conversation drifted from the psychic occurrence to her late friend's personal life and the difficulties she had encountered in adjusting to the world in which she lived. As she was speaking so freely about Linda being all by herself in the room she happened to turn her head and saw the flame in the heater slowly die out as if someone had just turned it off, yet no one had been near it. At that point she felt a sense of acute anger and a presence beyond her own. Elaine started to cry into the telephone. Her minister friend urged her to hang up and run for it, but even that she was completely unable to do. She knew that her late friend had come to listen in on the conversation about her and that she resented it. A few moments later her minister friend and his wife came running into the apartment. At that point Elaine was able to let go of the telephone and fall to the floor. Linda has not returned since. To this day Elaine regrets having gossiped about her late friend in view of that friend's help on the previous occasion. She remembers the old adage "de mortibus nihil nisi bonum," meaning when you speak of the dead speak only of good things.

The other experience which Elaine cannot ever completely forget occurred not long after the first one. She had an increasing feeling that one of her children would pass on soon. This went on for about a year and caused a mental condition which she found hard to cope with. Somehow she managed to live a normal life in spite of it. On April 2, 1958, she happened to be taking a dozen 4-H Club girls to a fabric shop to look for yard goods. It was 5:15 in the afternoon when she suddenly panicked. Without adequate explanation she rushed the girls in her care to the car and drove like a madwoman toward her home. One mile before she reached her home she passed an ambulance going in the opposite direction, and at that instant she knew that her four-year-old son Scott was already dead. She drove into her street, where her neighbors stood in groups crying and talking. Her fears were confirmed. Someone offered to drive her to the hospital. No one had yet told her exactly what had occurred. Later she learned that the boy had been alive but had died shortly after at the hospital. He had drowned. Apparently, she was told by her husband, he had jumped into a creek after their dog to rescue him. When she was told this, Elaine got very angry and did not wish to speak about it. Why were they all lying to her, she wondered, when she knew so much better what had actually happened. For the next three days she stayed in seclusion. Then the evening after her little boy's funeral she gathered up some of his toys and carried them across the street to some of his little friends. As she did so she suddenly knew that a little boy playmate of her son's by the name of Warren had pushed her boy into the creek. Returning home, she confronted her husband with the explanation, and he had no choice but to confirm it. Several times later she felt her little boy's presence although she could not see him. She felt no unhappiness with the little spirit yet wondered whether she should tell him that he had passed on in case he was not aware of it. Then a year after his passing, in September, when he was to have started school she felt him very strongly. A school bus was passing the house when she suddenly heard her dead little boy say to her, "I want to go to school." Without thinking about what she was doing she heard herself reply, "But you can't, darling, you're dead." Since then all has been quiet around Elaine's house. She hopes her little boy has found another school of his own over there where he now lives.

Jeffrey Oromaner is an electrical engineer by profession and because of his training not easily given to the acceptance of occult phenomena. He and his family moved into a newly built house on Sharp View Avenue in Houston on November 15, 1968. He was the first occupant of the house. His professional connection with a large computer company makes it necessary for Mr. Oromaner to travel frequently. At such times his wife is alone with their two children. The chain of events which made Mr. Oromaner wonder about poltergeists in his new home began with the sudden appearance of two large stuffed animals belonging to his three-year-old daughter. The animals had been missing for two weeks and no amount of searching had turned them up. Suddenly they reappeared in a most conspicuous place where they could not possibly have been overlooked. While the Oromaner family was still debating this phenomenon something else occurred. Mr. Oromaner was out of town and his wife and a fourteen-year-old baby-sitter spent the night in the downstairs bedroom of the house with the two children. While downstairs they heard a tremendous amount of walking and moving about upstairs. Immediately assuming that someone had entered the house they called the police. The police came and found nothing amiss. As soon as the police had left, the walking upstairs resumed. Mrs. Oromaner and the sitter were too frightened to do anything about it during the night but as soon as morning came they went directly into the children's bedroom upstairs. There they discovered that a table with the boy's electric train on it had moved clear across his large walk-in closet. No one had been upstairs during the night, nor had any human agency made these changes in the room. The following day Mr. Oromaner returned from his trip. He took the report less than seriously and teased his family about it, but when he awoke the next morning he was not so sure of the whole thing. In his daughter's room someone had taken a shelf down from among three shelves hanging on the wall. All the small stuffed animals that had been on that shelf were scattered around the room. Needless to add the girl had not done this, nor had anyone else been in the room during that time. A few days later Mr. Oromaner had to leave town again for a few days. Thoroughly frightened by now, his wife decided to ask two friends, two fourteen-year-old girls, to stay the night with her. Again they were awakened around two o'clock in the morning by the footsteps of someone walking upstairs. They also heard the boy's window being opened. Since they were all downstairs, including the kids, they decided to barricade themselves in the downstairs bedroom, forcing a heavy dresser in front of the door. Then they went to sleep with somewhat mixed feelings. When they awoke the next morning they discovered that the door to the bedroom was cracked about six inches across.

The following day Mr. Oromaner returned. He listened with somewhat more concern to what had happened in his absence. His wife went to bed early because of a cold. He remained downstairs alone watching television until about 11:30 p.m. Everything was in its proper place. He locked up and went to bed. Awakening the next morning, he noticed that two candle holders and a flower arrangement had been taken off the mantel of the fireplace, along with a ceramic leopard from atop the television, and that all these objects were arranged perfectly on the fireplace. He had not done any such thing nor had anyone else been in the room who could have done this. No one, that is, of flesh and blood. He immediately checked every window in the house, every door and every chain lock; nothing had been tampered with. At this point Mr. Oromaner, despite his scientific training, became thoroughly convinced of the reality of the phenomena in his house. As if in response to his open-minded attitude toward the occurrences they materialized now with greater frequency. An artificial weeping willow four feet high and rather heavy was moved six feet and lifted up to the first stair of the staircase. All without the help of human hands. Mr. Oromaner's pool balls were scattered and hidden all over his poolroom as if they had been Easter eggs. A flower arrangement was removed from a dresser and found on the floor right next to it without natural cause. Their clock radio was switched on by itself three times in a way that was different from the time he and his wife would have set. It was his custom to turn off all lights before going to bed. Nevertheless, more than once did Mr. Oromaner find the upstairs lights on when he was quite sure that he had not turned the switch prior to going to bed.

One Sunday afternoon his wife was taking a nap in the middle of their king-size bed. Mr. Oromaner was about ten feet away in another room when he heard the telephone fall off the table next to the bed. He assumed that the telephone had been close to the edge and had somehow fallen off but on checking realized that this could not have happened by natural means. He replaced the receiver and went back to the other room. Five minutes later he heard the telephone being violently knocked off the table again, and he ran into the bedroom only to find it stretched the length of its cord on the floor. During all this commotion his wife had been asleep.

At that point Mr. Oromaner requested my assistance in

clearing up the matter. Unfortunately his company transferred him to California before I could look into the origin of the strange occurrences at his house on Sharp View Avenue. The new occupants of the house have so far not complained about any unusual goings on. A written request by Mr. Oromaner to the new owners concerning such matters has remained unanswered, so one can only assume that the new owners have nothing to report or do not care to discuss it. What makes the case even more puzzling is the fact that no ghosts have disturbed the peace of the Oromaner family in their new location in California.

The old Howard home on South Main Street in Henderson, Texas, is a southern mansion of the kind that is so numerous throughout the South. In 1851 the mansion was erected by a certain James L. Howard on land he paid $100 for. It is the oldest brick home in town. Today it belongs to the Heritage Association and is being maintained as a museum, with visitors coming not only from other parts of Texas but even from abroad. The house has three stories and six rooms, and each room has a fireplace of its own. Four columns adorn the front of it. Perhaps the most remarkable thing about the house is the fact that every room has a fireplace, some of them very large old-fashioned fireplaces of the kind you rarely see any more. The stairs have banisters made of the highest grade walnut.

When the Howards built this home they stated proudly, to anyone who would hear it, "God Almighty Himself could not tear it down because it was so well built." Even the worst storm seemingly could not touch the house. There is the account of a particularly horrifying electrical storm when a streak of lightning hit one of the corner columns, causing only slight damage. One of the Howard brothers ran out into the yard, looked up into the sky and shook his fist and said, "See. I told you that you couldn't tear down my house." With so large and outstanding a mansion in a small town, it is only natural that legends would crop up around it, some of which are true and some are not. One of them making the rounds concerns a murder in the house. The present owners, the Rusk County Heritage Association, has checked into it and found that an accident and not a murder had occurred. The accident concerns a member of the Howards named Pat Howard who lost his life in an accident in the home. In fact the descendants of the Howards went to great length to explain again and again that Pat Howard died of an accident and that the shooting that took his life was not murder in any sense of the word. Of course where there is smoke there is sometimes fire. Was the family merely trying to kill the story, or were they correcting the facts? I have never been to the Henderson mansion but have talked with people who have been there, so my account must of necessity be second hand. In 1905 Mrs. M. A. Howard and Dore Howard, being alone, decided to sell the house to a certain Mrs. M. A. Dickinson. Mrs. Howard was then in ill health. The sale did not go down well with her children and the rest of the family, who would have preferred to have the house stay family property. It seems incredible today that such an imposing house could be sold for $1500, but, of course, that was a lot more money in 1905 than it is today. Still, even for 1905, $1500 was very little money for a house of this kind. It seems strange therefore that the sale was made in this manner. The sale of the house from the Howard family to an outsider took the town by surprise. No one had surmised that it could be for sale, especially not for such a low price. The house had a reputation as an historical landmark. Sam Houston himself slept there many times, since he was a cousin of the Howards. In 1950 the house passed from the Dickinson family to Hobart Bryce, who in 1961 deeded the property to the Historical Association. One of the townspeople who had spent much effort in restoring the old house and who had been active on behalf of the fund-raising committee was a certain Carl Jaggers. Partly due to his efforts and those of others, the house is now in excellent condition again and open to visitors as a museum. My attention was drawn to it when I appeared on a television program in nearby Tyler, Texas. The lady who interviewed me, Jane Lassiter, provided me with much of the material about the Henderson house.

While the controversy among the townspeople concerning the restoration of the house was going on and there was some doubt whether the house could be saved or had to be torn down, no one had the time or inclination to look into any possible ghostly manifestations at the house. But as soon as the matter had quieted down and the house was safe from the wreckers' tools and perhaps because of the renewed quiet in the atmosphere something did occur that had not been observed before. Maia Jaggers was one of those who served as honorary guides around the house, particularly during the weekends, when there were more visitors than during the week. She would act as hostess to those who came to look at the house. One Sunday afternoon in the winter of 1968, she had just finished showing the house to a group of visitors and was quite alone in it for the moment. She found herself downstairs looking toward the stairway leading to the upper stories. At that precise moment she saw a woman materialize before her eyes. Seemingly solid, or almost so, it was clearly a woman of a past age. As she looked closely at the apparition she realized that it was the ghost of Mrs. Howard herself. As soon as Maia Jaggers and the ghost had come face to face the apparition floated up the stairway and disappeared. She has not been seen since that time. Could it be that a grateful Mrs. Howard wanted the one person directly connected with the salvage of her home made aware of her continued existence in it? Was her presence in what was once her home caused by a belated regret at having sold out to others against the wishes of her family? If you are ever in Henderson, Texas, be sure and drop in on Mrs. Howard's house. Sale or no sale, she seems to be quite at home in it still.

Grace Trotter lives in Dallas and is in her middle thirties. She is the author of several novels for young girls published by leading houses. In recent years, however, she has become more and more interested in the occult, partly because of an experience that opened her eyes to the continuance of life after death. She contacted me after she had read my book of that title to tell me of a visitation that, in a manner of speaking, had changed her outlook entirely. In 1965 Miss Trotter, who writes under the professional name of Nancy Paschal, suffered the loss of her father in July, and in October that of her mother too. The double passing left a deep imprint on Miss Trotter. Her mother had died on a Friday and was buried the following Monday morning.

That afternoon, after her friends had left the house, Miss Trotter lay down to rest in her house and fell asleep. She was awakened from deep slumber about an hour later by something or someone whose presence she felt in the room. She opened her eyes and looked straight into her mother's face. This was no dream but a fully materialized apparition. She noticed that her mother was dressed in white, and while she was observing her in awe her mother came over to her and kissed her. She felt the imprint of her lips quite clearly. At the foot of her bed stood a smaller woman, a brunette, dressed in red. Grace Trotter also recognized the other woman as her mother's mother, her own grandmother, even though she had died many years before Grace was born. She had been familiar with her appearance from a large picture which had been in the house. Not a word was spoken and the entire experience lasted perhaps five or ten minutes. After it was over Miss Trotter wondered whether she had not been asleep after all when it occurred. There was a certain wish to believe and a deep understanding for the need for this occurrence to have taken place, but at the same time her rational and scientific mind wanted to be sure that that which she had experienced was real. She did not have to wait long for additional confirmation. Two weeks later she awoke one morning and saw her mother again coming from the door. Now Grace Trotter realized that her mother did not look her age, that is to say the age she was when she passed on. Again she wore a beautiful dress. The other woman who had been in the first visitation was along this time too. But what amazed Grace Trotter more was the fact that her mother carried in her arms what appeared to be a six-month-old baby. It came to her in a flash that the baby was she, for she had been six months of age when her mother was twenty-four. The picture of her mother holding her own self as a baby was the additional proof of identity Miss Trotter needed. The apparitions faded quickly, but the imprint they left behind has stayed with her ever since. As a professional writer and poet she felt herself impelled to put down on paper what the experience had meant to her, and she has asked me to reproduce that beautiful poem called *Safe Passage* in this account. Here it is:

SAFE PASSAGE

By Nancy Paschal

My mother passed on a Friday
Just twenty minutes after Thursday midnight.
I was alone with her when she drew the breath
That was final. And it was right
That it was free from pain and peaceful, dear Lord.
But grief caught me like blinding light.
I couldn't see my way without her—
My counsellor, my friend, my own sweet mother.
She was a real young eighty-nine
And I had loved her all of sixty-five years,
But giving her up was so hard
That I couldn't stop the hurting or the tears.
She was buried Monday morning.
That afternoon, after all my friends had left,
I lay on my bed and fell asleep.
In an hour, when I woke up sad and bereft,
Mother was standing beside me.
She bent over and kissed my lips, quick and deft
And loving, as she always was.
I gazed into her smiling face
And it was young—not more than twenty-four.
Her body looked strong, with beauty and grace.
One morning two weeks later I woke early
And saw her again, coming in at the door.

She had a six-months-old baby in her arms.
I had been six months old when she was twenty-four,
So the baby was me.
She brought my baby-self back for me to see,
To prove that she still lived and cared
And that death is only a passageway.
The spirit of life everlasting dared
To show itself as plain as day.
Death is a safe passageway.

One of the most popular legends in American ghostlore is the "hitchhiking ghost story." It has been told to me many times by people in many states. Carl Carmer has immortalized the hitchhiking girl ghost in one of his books and there is no doubt that the legend is part of traditional American folklore. Consequently I treat further variations of this tale with extreme caution, if not outright skepticism. Basically the story concerns someone driving at night who is flagged down by a stranger in the road. The stranger is always a girl, always beautiful, and she always wears unusual clothes such as an evening gown or other formal attire. She asks for a lift home, and of course the motorist obliges. The girl then gets in and sits in the back, and when the motorist reaches the destination requested by the girl he turns around and lo and behold there is no one in his back seat. His curiosity has been aroused. He rings the doorbell at the house in question, someone opens the door, and when he describes the girl hitchhiker he is told that the lady in question died many years ago and that this has happened before. So much for the traditional hitchhiking ghost.

I am indebted to Chuck Meegan of the Dallas *Morning News* and to a reader by the name of Joanne Darr of Dallas for a story which seems to run in a similar pattern but has the ring of truth to it. Miss Darr moved to Dallas in 1962 and soon after her arrival heard about the ghost of White Rock Lake. Being somewhat interested in the occult, she questioned those who told her of this particular apparition. The lake is man-made and is now in a residential area, part of a city park. The alleged ghost lived in that area. In former years there were some very fine homes close to the water, and in the thirties these homes were famous for garden parties and boating excursions on the lake. According to tradition, during one of these parties a boat tipped over and a young girl and her fiancé were drowned. In other accounts it is only the girl who was drowned and her ghost is now wandering around looking for her fiancé. She wears evening clothes and tries to hitch a ride back home to Gaston Avenue in the Lakewood area, which is about three miles' distance. But according to local tradition she simply disappears before she gets there. According to some other accounts she disappears immediately after she is given the ride to where she wants to go. Her benefactor then goes to that address and meets her grandfather, who explains the situation to him.

All this seemed terribly ridiculous to Miss Darr. She discussed it with a local friend, who didn't find it so amusing as she did. Her grandfather had been fishing just after dark not long before, and as he looked out onto the lake he clearly saw a human shape floating above the water. He didn't catch many fish that night. The story kept bothering Miss Darr and she did some further research. Through material in the Dallas *Morning News* she made contact with a woman who worked for Neiman-Marcus as the head of the advertising department. The lady was quite obliging in recounting her unusual experience. This happened in the late thirties or early forties, she explained, and it was in the early morning when she and her boyfriend, who later became her husband, were driving home and passing the lake. Suddenly they noticed a girl crawling up the embankment next to the road. They stopped the car in order to help her. She was dripping wet and wore a blue evening dress. She explained that she lived on Gaston just past Lakewood and that she had been in an accident on the lake. They offered to drive her home and the girl got into the back seat of the car. Since the woman and her boyfriend were rather tired at the end of a long evening, they didn't feel like talking to the stranger, and the girl also remained quiet in the back seat. When they were nearing the Lakewood area the woman turned around to see if the girl was all right. To her amazement the stranger had completely vanished. The car they were driving was a two-door sedan, and no one could have gotten in or out through the windows.

The address where the girl once lived has since been turned into an apartment house. Nevertheless, every year, especially in the spring or fall during the height of the social season, various people claim to have seen her there. The story appealed to one of Miss Darr's friends, who decided to do a little bit of ghost hunting on his own. He went to the general area where the figure of the girl had been observed in the past and waited. To his surprise he saw a white form standing in the road. When he came closer to her she dissolved. Evidently the girl of White Rock Lake is still trying to hitch a ride home.

Sylvia W. is in her late twenties, has been married twice and has lived a full and normally exciting life. Since the age of eight she has had precognitive experiences, warnings, feelings about impending events, many of which have come true, and psychic dreams. She has always accepted the importance of ESP in her life and never had any fears of the so-called occult. But recently something has happened in her life that has her stumped. She has fallen in love with a widower, Albert, whose wife and infant daughter were killed in a motorcar accident in 1961. Albert himself was slightly injured in the same accident. Albert's wife herself had had a premonition of the impending accident and had told him so. Moreover, three days after her death she appeared before him and assured him that she would always be with him and take care of him. Before her passing she had requested that should she die he should not remarry. He did not promise this but she had earnestly requested it.

As soon as Albert had gotten over the shock of his wife's untimely passing he began to mingle socially once again. Despite increased social interest he remained single. However, when he met Sylvia they became involved with each other in a love relationship. They had originally met because her house was rented from his company. They dated for about six months, and the first four months of their relationship was undisturbed and harmonious. But then strange things started to happen and they couldn't help noticing it. Strange noises and movements occurred both in her house and in his house. That was not surprising since they spent time in both. There were knockings on the door and when they opened it there was no one there. This happened mainly late at night. Then there were sounds of someone walking in the next room or heavy objects seemingly dropping to the floor. Upon investigation they found nothing to substantiate the noises. On occasion the blinds would open by themselves or a book would move of its own volition and open by itself to a certain page while the room in which this happened was closed off and no one had access to it. Apparently someone was trying to convey messages to Albert, for the books were marked at different passages. When they read one of the passages in a particular novel that had been left in a conspicuous spot so that they could not overlook it, they realized who was behind the phenomena. The passage in the book dealt with a female competitor who was domineering; about honest love, and about one partner being "from another world." And one passage referred to someone having seen the light.

Fantastic as it seemed at first, they realized that the dead wife was trying to break up their romance from the beyond. When they were together during the night there was a knocking on the window. Albert got up to investigate outside. After he had left the bedroom Sylvia rose and looked out onto the patio through the blinds.

The lights were on in the patio and she assumed that Albert was checking that area of the house. Also, she clearly heard the door to the kitchen open and close and lock itself. After Albert returned she learned that he had not even been in the back of the house where the patio and kitchen are located. He had been to the front only. In the middle of the night they tried to go over the phenomena and make some sense out of them. In listing them they realized that the disturbances had started just about the time Albert had declared his love for Sylvia. Moreover, Sylvia had just borrowed an object that had belonged to Albert's first wife. It was a typewriter. She had left it on the floor only to find it moved the following morning from the floor and back to the shelf where it had originally been. No one had been near it during the night. That is to say, no one of flesh and blood. What were they to do? Pending a visit to me I explained that they must address the deceased woman and explain the facts of life to her or perhaps the facts of "after life." Only by making her understand the error of her ways could they hope to release her from her compulsion and themselves from her interference. I have not heard from Sylvia since then and can only hope that it worked.

I met Mrs. Ann B. the last time I was lecturing in Houston. She is a middle-class housewife. Her husband is an electrician and doesn't put much stock in her occult experiences. He discourages them. Nevertheless, all through the years Ann has had flashes, premonitions and visions, most of which later became objective reality. She is one of those Texans who have the gift of second sight in a very clear way and would like to use it constructively to help others if not herself. Among the most interesting experiences reported by Ann B. is an incident which occurred in 1957. At the time she was living in a small town near Houston. She was having recurrent dreams in which she saw her husband being hurt. Specifically she saw a flash of fire and her husband came rolling out of it across a wooden floor. He seemed to be in terrible pain. Since she had the dream a number of times she decided to discuss it with him, but he would not listen. Then the dream stopped. A few days after she had had this dream for the last time her husband had to go to a nearby town to do some electrical work in a church. While he was doing this, two high-tension wires accidentally touched and her husband was caught by the current. In order to get out of it he rolled across a wooden floor and his hands and arms were badly burned. On August 1, 1960, in the evening, she had a vision of her brother-in-law who lived in another city in Texas. They had not been in touch lately and there really wasn't any emotional reason for her to have the vision at this time. Nevertheless, she suddenly saw his head and shoulders and he seemed to be ascending. The strangest part of this vision was that there were pieces of broken metal floating all around him. She noticed that he had a most peaceful look on his face and knew that he had been killed in an accident. She told her husband so, but it wasn't until the next morning that the telephone rang and they were told that the brother-in-law had been killed in a plane crash.

The interest in mind development classes is considerable in the south today. From this a new crop of non-professional mediums will emerge people who understand that the gift is natural and not to be shunned. Some time ago I wanted to go to the Alamo with a reputable professional medium to do some research on the spot where so much history was made. Although I addressed the current custodians of this shrine twice and my letter was never returned, I was never given permission to do so nor did I receive an answer. Possibly ordinary people are a little ahead of those who fancy themselves representatives of public opinion. I have received many invitations from Texans to come and visit their haunted houses or to listen to the account of their extraordinary experiences with extrasensory perception, so I can forget the Alamo.

THE DEVIL IN TEXAS

I am frequently asked to comment on poltergeists, or noisy ghosts, a term derived from the German and somehow conjuring up the image of violent physical activity beyond the pale of ordinary understanding. Poltergeists have been generally considered the work of youngsters in a house—youngsters below the age of puberty, when their physical energies have not yet been channeled either sexually or occupationally and are therefore free to play pranks on others in the household. The majority of parapsychologists consider poltergeists the unconscious expression of such repressed feelings, attention getters on the part of young people, and do not connect them to supernormal beings such as spirit entities or any other form of outside influence. I, however, have investigated dozens of cases involving poltergeists where physical objects have been moved or moved seemingly by their own volition and found that another explanation might be the true one. In each case, to be sure, there were young people in the household, or sometimes retarded adults. I discovered, for instance, that a retarded adult has the same kind of suppressed kinetic energy that is capable of being tapped by outside forces to perform the physical phenomena as the unused energy of youngsters. I also discovered that in each and every case with which I came in contact personally there had been some form of unfinished business in the house or on the grounds on which the house stood. Sometimes this involved a previous building on the same spot. At other times it involved the same building in which the activities took place. But in each instance there was some form of psychic entity present, and it is my conviction that the entity from beyond the physical world was responsible for the happenings, using, of course, the physical energy in the young people or in the retarded adult. Thus, to me, poltergeists are the physical activities of ghosts expressed through the psychic powers within young people or retarded older people, but directed solely by outside entities no longer in the flesh. This link between the physical energies of living persons and the usually demented minds of dead persons produces the physical phenomena known as poltergeist activities which can be very destructive, sometimes threatening, sometimes baffling to those who do not understand the underlying causes.

The purpose of these physical activities is always to get the attention of living persons or perhaps to annoy them for personal reasons. The mentality behind this phenomenon is somewhere between the psychotic and the infantile, but at all times far from emotionally and mentally normal. But it can still be dealt with on the same basis as I deal with ordinary hauntings. That is to say, the cause of the activities must be understood before a cure for them can be found. Making contact with the troubled entity in the non-physical world is, of course, the best way. When that is not possible, a shielding device has to be created for the living to protect them from the unwanted poltergeist activities. In the well-publicized Seaford, Long Island, case a few years ago, a young boy in the household was held responsible for the movement of objects in plain daylight. Even so astute an investigator as Dr. Karlis Osis of the American Society of Psychical Research, who was then working for Parapsychology Foundation of New York City, could not discern the link between the boy's unconscious thought and the unseen, but very real, psychic entities beyond the world of the flesh. In his report he intimates that the activities were due to the unconscious desires of the youngster to be noticed and to get the sort of attention his unconscious self craved. I was not involved in the Seaford case personally although I was familiar with it, having discussed the matter with Mr. Herman, the boy's father. I did not enter the case because certain aspects of it suggested publicity seeking on the part of the family, and at any rate others in my field had already entered the case. I saw no reason to crowd the scene, but I did go into the background of the house with the help of medium Ethel Johnson Meyers independently of the investigation conducted by Dr. Osis. For what it may be worth at this late date, my sitting with Mrs. Meyers disclosed that an Indian burial ground had existed on the very site of the Seaford house and that the disturbances were due to the fact that the house had been erected on that spot. They had not occurred earlier since no physical medium lived in the house. When the young man reached the age of puberty, or nearly so, his energies were available to those wishing to manifest, and it was then that the well-publicized movement of objects occurred.

Similarly, two years ago a case attracted public attention in the city of Rosenheim, Bavaria. A young lady working for an attorney in that city was somehow able to move solid objects by her very presence. A long list of paranormal phenomena was recorded by reputable witnesses, including the attorney himself. Eventually Dr. Hans Bender of the University of Freiburg entered the case and after investigation pronounced it a classical poltergeist situation. He too did not link the activity with any outside entity that might have been present on the premises from either this house or a previous one standing on the spot. It seems to me that at the time great haste was taken to make sure that a physical or temporal solution could be put forward, making it unnecessary to link the phenomena with any kind of spirit activity.

But perhaps the most famous of all poltergeist cases, the classical American case, is the so-called Bell Witch of Tennessee. This case goes back to the 1820s and even so illustrious a witness as Andrew Jackson figures in the proceedings. Much has been written and published about the Bell Witch of Tennessee. Suffice it to say here that it involved the hatred of a certain woman for a farmer named John Bell. This relationship resulted in a post-mortem campaign of hatred and destructiveness ultimately costing the lives of two people. In the Bell Witch case of Tennessee the entire range of physical phenomena usually associated with poltergeistic activities was observed.

Included were such astounding happenings as the appearance or disappearance of solid objects into and out of thin air; strange smells and fires of unknown origin; slow deliberate movement of objects in plain sight without seeming physical source; and voices being heard out of the air when no one present was speaking. Anyone studying the proceedings of this case would notice that the phenomena were clearly the work of a demented individual. Even though a certain degree of cunning and cleverness is necessary to produce them, the reasoning behind or, rather, the lack of reasoning, clearly indicates a disturbed mind. All poltergeist activities must therefore be related to the psychotic, or, at the very least, schizophrenic state of mind of the one causing them. As yet we do not clearly understand the relationship between insanity and free energies capable of performing acts seemingly in contradiction of physical laws, but there seems to be a very close relationship between these two aspects of the human personality. When insanity exists certain energies become free and are capable of roaming at will at times and of performing feats in contradiction to physical laws. When the state of insanity in the mind under discussion is reduced to normalcy these powers cease abruptly.

I have, on occasion, reported cases of hauntings and ghostly activities bordering upon or including some poltergeist activities. Generally we speak of them as physical phenomena. A case in point is the haunted house belonging to Mr. and Mrs. John Smythe of Rye, New York. The phenomena in this house included such physical activities as doors opening by themselves, footsteps, the sound of chains rattling, ashtrays flying off the table by themselves, and, most frightening of all, a carving knife taking off by itself on a Sunday morning in full view of two adult sane people and flinging itself at their feet, not to hurt them but to call attention to an existing unseen entity in the house. These are, of course, the kind of activities present in poltergeist cases, but they are merely a fringe activity underlining the need for communication. They are not the entire case, nor are they as disorganized and wanton as the true poltergeist cases. In the case of Rye, New York, the physical activities followed long-time mental activities such as apparitions and impressions of a presence. The physical phenomena were primarily used here to make the message more urgent. Not so with the true poltergeist case, where there is no possibility of mental communication simply because the causing person is incapable of actual thinking. In such a case all energies are channeled toward destructive physical activity and there is neither the will nor the ability to give mental impressions to those capable of receiving them, since the prime mover of these activities is so filled with hatred and the desire to manifest in the physical world that he or she will not bother with so rational an activity as a thought message.

It is therefore difficult to cope with cases of this kind since there is no access to reasoning, as there is in true ghost cases when a trance medium can frequently make contact with the disturbed and disturbing entity in the house and slowly, but surely, bring it back to the realm of reason. With the true poltergeist case nothing of the sort can be established and other means to solve it have to be found. It is therefore quite natural that anyone who becomes the victim of such activities and is not familiar with them or with what causes them will be in a state of panic, even to the point of wanting to abandon his property and run for his life.

On September 1, 1968, I was contacted by a gentleman by the name of L. H. Beaird. He wrote to me from Tyler, Texas, requesting that I help him understand some of the extraordinary happenings that had made his life hell on earth during the period of three years between 1965 and 1968. Through his daughter who was married in Austin he learned of my work with ghosts and finally concluded that only someone as familiar with the subject as I could shed light on the mysterious happenings in his home. He had purchased their home in 1964, but after three years of living with a poltergeist and fighting a losing battle for survival he decided that his sanity and survival were more important, and in 1968 he sold it again, losing everything he had put into it. The move, however, was a fortuitous one, for the new home turned out to be quiet and peaceful. Once Mr. Beaird got his bearings again and learned to relax once more he decided to investigate what had occurred during the previous three years and find some sort of answer to this extraordinary problem.

I had never heard of Tyler before and decided to look it up on the map. It turned out to be a city of about 60,000 inhabitants also known as the "rose capital" because of the large number of horticultural activities in the area. Tyler is connected with Dallas and Houston by a local airline and lies about halfway between Dallas and Shreveport, Louisiana. It has one television station, one newspaper and some pleasant ordinary citizens going about their various businesses. The people of Tyler whom I got to know a little after my visit later on are not concerned with such things as the occult. In fact, anyone trying to lecture on the subject would do so in empty halls.

Howard Beaird works in a nearby hospital and also runs a rubber stamp shop in which he has the company of his wife and more orders than he can possibly fill. Their son, Andy, was enrolled in barber school at the time of my visit and presumably is now cutting people's hair to everyone's satisfaction somewhere in Texas. The big local hotel is called the Blackstone and it is about the same as other big hotels in small towns. Everything is very quiet in Tyler, Texas, and you can really sleep at night. There is a spirit of not wanting to change things, of letting sleeping dogs lie as much as possible, pervading the town, and I have the distinct impression that cases such as the poltergeist case were not exactly welcome subjects for discussion over a drink at the local bar.

It must be held to Mr. Beaird's credit that despite the indications of small-town life he felt compelled to make inquiries into the extraordinary happenings in his life, to look into them without fear and with great compassion for those involved—his wife and son. Others in his position might have buried the matter and tried to forget it. This is particularly important since Mr. Beaird is reasonably prosperous, does business with his neighbors and has no intention of leaving Tyler. To ask me for an investigation was tantamount to stirring things up, but Beaird took this calculated risk because he could not live with the knowledge of what he had observed and not know what had caused it.

At the time of our correspondence in September of 1968 the phenomena had already ended as abruptly as they had come. This too is typical of genuine poltergeist activities, since they depend solely on the available free energies of living people. As will be seen in the course of my investigation, that energy became no longer available when the principals were removed from the house. There are other factors involved of course. It is not as simple as plugging in on a power line, but in essence poltergeist activities depend not only on the desire of the disturbing entity to manifest but also on the physical condition of the unconscious part of those whom they wish to use as power supplies.

The house which the Beairds had to leave under pressure from their poltergeists is on Elizabeth Street. It is a one-story ranch-type dwelling, pleasant enough to look at and about fourteen or fifteen years old. The new owners are not particularly keen on the history of their house, and it is for that reason that I am keeping confidential the actual location, but the house has not been altered in any way since it has been sold to Mr. M. and his family. One enters the house through a porch that is located somewhat above the road. There is a garage and a steep driveway to the right of the porch. Once one is inside the house one is in the living room with a den to the left and a dining area to the right. Beyond the living room are the kitchen and a rather long room leading directly to a breakfast room. On the extreme left are two bedrooms. To the right of the house behind the garage is the workshop, which, in the period when Mr. Beaird owned the house, was used as such. There is also a concrete slab separating the shop from the garage proper, and the garage contains a ladder leading up to the attic.

Howard Beaird, sixty-five years of age, is a pleasant man with a soft Texas accent, polite, firm, and obliging in his manner. He was overjoyed when I expressed an interest in his case and promised to cooperate in every way. In order to get a better understanding of the extraordinary happenings at Tyler I asked that he dictate in his own words the story of those three years in the house that had come to be three years of unrelenting terror. The principals in this true account besides Howard Beaird are his wife, Johnnie, whom he has always called John; a daughter named Amy who lives in another city and was in no way involved in the strange experiences at Tyler; and a son, Andy, now nineteen, who shared all of the unspeakable horror of the experiences between 1965 and the early part of 1968 with his parents. Most of the others mentioned in his account have been dead for several years. A few are still alive, and there are some names in this account Mr. Beaird has never heard of. Here then is his own account of what occurred in the little house on Elizabeth Street in Tyler, Texas:

"My story begins late in 1962, which marked the end of nearly thirty-nine years of employment with the same company. During the last twenty years of that time John worked in the same office with me; in fact her desk was only a few feet from mine. We were both retired during September of 1962.

"John had always been an excellent employee, but devoted much more time to her work than the company required for any one person. She would never take a vacation, and was rarely away from her job for more than an occasional half-day at a time, mainly, I think, because she would trust no one with her work. I cannot say when her mind began to show signs of being disturbed, although as I think back on it today, she had acted a little strangely for several years prior to the time of our retirement. This, however, did not affect her work in any way; in fact she was even more precise in it than ever, and I suppose I just could not bring myself to admit that there was anything wrong with her mind. At any rate, during the next twelve months she began to act more abnormally than ever, especially when at home, until finally it was necessary that she enter a mental institution. Although the doctors there were reluctant to release her, they did not seem to be having any success in whatever treatment they were giving her, so I asked for her release after about three months. Being of very modest means I naturally had to obtain employment as soon as possible, but after working about three months in another city I felt that it was most urgent that I move my family from Grand Saline, Texas, to some other place, believing that the mere change of environment would play a big part in helping John to get well. So about the middle of 1964 we moved to Tyler, Texas, a place where John had always said she would like to live. We bought a house, and after about a month I obtained employment which, in addition to a sideline business I had begun a few years before, gave us a satisfactory, if not affluent, living. For almost a year John did seem to be better; she would go places with Andy and me, to the Little League baseball games in which Andy played, to the movies occasionally, sometimes to bowling alleys and a miniature golf course, but all of a sudden she stopped.

"She had not actually kept house since we made the move and had not cooked a single meal for Andy or me. About this time she started walking to a drugstore in a nearby shopping center for breakfast, and then in the late afternoon just before I would get home she would walk to a restaurant a few blocks away for the evening meal, usually by herself. A little later she began calling a taxi nearly every morning to go to a different place for breakfast: once to a downtown hotel; once way out on the other side of town to a roadside restaurant on the Mineola Highway, and to many other places within the course of a few weeks. Always in the evenings though she would go to the restaurant near our home. She would come home usually just after I arrived, and would change clothes and stay in her room from then on. She would get up very early in the morning, about five o'clock, something *she had never done* during our entire married life. For the past few years she insisted that people were spying on her, and finally, when I did not agree with her, she accused of me of being at the head of this group set out to torment her, and even said that I had television cameras set up in the house to spy on her.

"John smoked almost incessantly, every kind of cigarette made, but later began to smoke little cigars the size of a cigarette, and still later started on the big regular ones that men smoke. Once she bought a small can of snuff. She had never used snuff before. This was a little while after she had begun to lay cigarettes down just anywhere, although there were plenty of ashtrays throughout the house. She also began putting lighted cigarettes on table tops, the arms of a divan, or even on the bed, and if Andy or I had not been there to put them out, no doubt the house would have eventually been burned down. She did burn holes in several sheets and in the mattress on her bed. When that happened I told her that she simply could not smoke any more. She did not protest. Andy and I searched the house and found cigarettes and matches everywhere. John had hidden them everywhere, inside a little table radio by removing the back, inside a flashlight where the batteries are supposed to be, in those little shoe pockets she had hanging in her closet, in a little opening at the end of the bathtub where a trap door in the closet exposes the pipes for repairs, under the mattress, inside pillow covers, and even in the dog house outdoors. We gathered up cigarettes, matches, and cigarette lighters every day when I got home and there is no telling how many we finally found and destroyed. Of course she would get more every day at the shopping center, and once we even found one of those little automatic rollers that a person can use to make his own cigarettes.

"Exactly what part John played in the frightening events that took place at our house I cannot say. I am convinced though, as is Amy, that there was some connection. The three years from late 1962 to the summer of 1965 preceded the most awesome, fantastic chain of events that the human mind can imagine. In fact, as these unbelievable episodes began to unfold before us I was beginning to doubt my own sanity. Andy, who was 13 at the time this began, shared with me every one of the horrible experiences, which started in midsummer of 1965 and lasted without interruption until near the end of 1966, when we were 'told' that they were over with, only to find that during the next fifteen months we were in for even worse things. If Andy had not been with me to substantiate these awful experiences I would have indeed considered myself hopelessly insane.

"The frightening events began to take place near the middle of 1965, about the time John quit going places with Andy and me. When at home she would stay in her bedroom and close the door and leave it closed after she went to bed. Andy and I slept in the same bed in another room.

"During our first year at this house we were not bothered by the usual summertime insects, so I did not bother to repair the screens needing fixing at that time. However, during July of 1965, Andy and I would go to bed, and as soon as we turned out the light we were plagued by hordes of June bugs of all sizes, which would hit us on our heads and faces, some glancing off on the floor, others landing on the bed, and some missing us entirely and smashing themselves against the metal window blinds. Night after night we fought these bugs in the dark, grabbing those that landed on the bed and throwing them against the blinds as hard as we could.

"Then we discovered that at least half of the bugs that hit us were *already dead,* in fact had been dead so long that they were crisp and would crumble between our fingers when we picked them up! I would get up and turn on the lights, and the raids would cease immediately; we could see no sign of them in the air . . . only those hundreds that littered the floor and bed. The instant I turned off the light, though, the air would be filled with bugs again, just as if someone were standing there ready to throw handfuls at us *as soon as it was dark.* One night I got up and swept and vacuumed the entire room, moved every piece of furniture away from the walls, dusted the backs of the dresser, chest and tables, and vacuumed the floor again. When I was through I could swear that there was not a living creature in that room other than Andy and me. I got some rags and stuffed them in the cracks beneath the closet door and the one leading from the room into the hall. The windows were closed. The room was *absolutely clean.* Andy was in bed, awake. I turned off the light. At that exact instant hundreds of bugs hit us!

"About this time John began to act more strangely than ever, doing things she would not dream of doing under ordinary circumstances. For example, I might look in my closet to get a shirt or a pair of trousers, and there would not be any there. I do not know what prompted me to do it, but I would go to John's closet, and there would be my clothes hanging alongside some of hers.

"At this time I had a rubber stamp shop in a room behind the garage, which was a part of the house, and I worked out there every night. There was no direct connection from the house. One had to go out the kitchen door into the garage and then through another door into the shop. On many occasions I would hear the kitchen door being opened, and would rush to the shop door to see who it was. No matter how hard I tried, though, I could never get there fast enough to see *anybody* . . . only my clothes, suits, shirts, etc., on hangers *just as they landed in the middle of the garage floor.*

"It was during the hottest part of summer while we had the air-conditioners running that other strange things took place for which we assumed John was responsible. Andy or I would suddenly find the bathroom wall heater lighted and the flames running out the top, with the door closed.

The room would be hot enough to burst into flames. John insisted that she had not lit the heater . . . that one of us had. After this had happened several times, I removed the handle that turns on the gas. A short time later, while I was out in the shop, Andy came running out and called me in. There was a bunch of paper towels stuffed into the heater where the burners are and they were on fire, some of them on the floor, burning. I then decided to turn off all the pilot lights in the house. This was on the weekend before Labor Day, and I did not know how I could possibly go to work on Tuesday following the holiday and leave John at home alone, since Andy would be in school. I had talked with Dr. Bankhead, a psychiatrist, and asked if I might put her in the hospital until I could determine what I would eventually be able to do with her, but the psychiatric wards were already running over, and he did not want to admit her as a patient. I decided to tell John that if she did 'any of those things' again I would have to put her in jail. Monday night she started waving a pistol around, so I called the police station and told them the predicament I was in. They said they would keep her until things could be settled and told me to bring her on down. She went without protest. When my lawyer returned he made appointments for her to be examined by two psychiatrists, after which I thought there would be no further question about the need for commitment, and she stayed at home that week. However, on the Monday following Labor Day she called her sister-in-law Mack in Daingerfield, Texas, about a hundred miles from Tyler, and asked if she could visit her at once. I was at work and knew nothing of this until Mack got to Tyler and asked if it would be all right for John to go with her. I objected, but my lawyer advised me that I should let her go, as she could be brought back for the commitment hearing, so they left that day for Daingerfield.

"A few days later John's lawyer had her examined by a psychiatrist again, and he finally said that she might benefit somewhat from getting a job, although she would have to undergo psychiatric treatment at various times in the future. It would be almost impossible to have her committed involuntarily, so we decided to just let things stand as they were. For the record, John's attorney insisted that I be examined by the same doctors who had examined her. The reports on me were favorable.

"Shortly after John had gone off to stay with Mack, Andy and I were lying in bed with the lights off, talking about the terrible things we had gone through. *Suddenly I heard a voice calling my name* . . . a high-pitched, falsetto voice that seemed to be coming from out in space. The voice said it was John, and although it sounded nothing at all like her, I am convinced it was, since she talked about several things that only she and I knew of. One was about some disagreeable words she had had with one of my sisters at the time of my father's death in 1950. She said that although my other sister had insulted her, she was good, and that she had forgiven her. Andy did not hear any part of this conversation. Apparently John, or the voice, could talk to either of us without the other hearing. I even suspected that Andy was doing the talking, and I held my fingers to his lips while listening to the voice. I knew then it could not have been coming from his lips.

"One night while I was lying on the bed and Andy was in the bathroom I heard his voice say 'goodbye,' though, just before he came to bed, and *he told me he had been talking with his mother*. During the following weeks we heard six other voices *from right out of nowhere,* all from people *who had been dead for some time*. I knew all but one of them while they were living. Two of them had always been friendly toward me, and both were old enough to be my mother. Andy also knew these two women and one of the men named George Swinney. This latter person was killed in an accident some time *after* he visited us 'by voice.' The other two women were mothers of friends of mine and both had died some time before we moved to Tyler. One was Mrs. Snow and the other was Mrs. Elliott, and theirs were the next two voices we heard after John had left, and they came to us about the time the visits by Henry Anglin started. He was the only one of the lot who gave us trouble to start with; in fact I am convinced that he is the one responsible for the bug raids and other awful things that happened to us.

"One of the work benches in my shop was against the wall dividing the shop and the kitchen, and at the bottom of the wall was an opening with a grill over it to handle the return air from the central heating system. For some reason the grill on the shop side had been removed, and by stooping down near the floor under the bench I could see much of what was going on in the kitchen. I worked in the shop every night, and when these 'ghosts' first began visiting us they would call my name, the voices seeming to come from the opening into the kitchen. I would stoop down and answer. At that time I would carry on lengthy conversations with all of them. Mrs. Snow and Mrs. Elliott were very friendly and seemed to want to give me all kinds of good advice. Henry Anglin was just the opposite. He was extremely mean and demanded that I do all sorts of things I would not do. When I refused, he would be very nasty. Once he got a can of insect spray we kept on the kitchen cabinet top and held it down at the opening to my shop. He would start spraying through the hole. He used a whole can of spray and in that little room I nearly suffocated. One cannot imagine what a feeling it is *to see a can of insect spray suspended in midair with apparently nothing holding it and to have it sprayed right in one's face!* When I went inside I could see the dents made by the edge of the can where he had banged it against the wall.

"About the middle of September 1965 the nightly bug raids began to taper off. We thought that we were going to get a few nights' sleep without fear. However, when we went to bed we would feel something moving on an arm or in our hair—*after* we had turned off the lights. We jumped up and found one or several *slugs* somewhere on us or on the bed. They are the ugliest, slimiest wormlike creatures that can be imagined, big at the head and tapering to a point toward their rear end. They have whiskers on each side of the head, and although they have eyes, they are not supposed to see very well, according to Andy, who, strangely enough, was studying them at school at that time. The large ones are as big as a Vienna sausage, about three inches long, and leave a silvery looking trail wherever they crawl. When the first few of these creatures appeared Andy thought they had clung to his shoes while he was playing in the yard and had gotten into the house that way. However, night after night the number of slugs increased, and we went through the same torture as with the bugs, only much worse. One cannot imagine how awful it is to wake up in the middle of the night and find oneself surrounded by a horde of slimy, ugly worms! Andy said that salt would dissolve the slugs. So we sprinkled salt all around the baseboard, around the bed legs, but still the slugs came *as soon as the lights were out.* A few nights later we were again bombarded with bugs . . . not June bugs this time, but the wood louse, the little bug about the size of a blackeyed pea. They have lots of tiny legs, will roll up into a round ball when touched, and are generally called pill bugs. I knew they could not fly, yet there they came, *hitting us just as if they were shot out of a gun,* at the exact moment we turned out the lights! Mixed in with these were some bugs I had never seen anywhere before, like a doodle bug but brown in color. I knew doodle bugs couldn't fly, and these things no more had wings than I did. Yet there they came, shooting through the air, and, just as the June bugs had done, they started out one or two at a time, until finally dozens began hitting us at once the moment the lights were out. I also found little pieces of clear material which looked like pieces of broken glass. I finally discovered that these pieces were making the loud noise against the blinds . . . some of them landed on the bed along with the peculiar bugs. I then washed off a piece about the size of a pea and tasted it; it was pure rock salt! I had not the slightest idea where it came from, as we certainly had had no use for any here. As baffling as the idea of bugs flying without wings was, it was no more so than rock salt sailing through the air with apparently nothing to propel it. There was absolutely no human being in the house except Andy and me.

"A day or two after John had left, I cleaned up her room thoroughly, moved every piece of furniture, swept, vacuumed, dusted, and made up the bed, putting on a spread that came nearly to the floor. A few days after the second series of bug raids, Andy called me into John's room. He raised up the spread, and there under the bed was a conglomeration of objects, among which was a ten-pound sack of rock salt, most of which had been poured in a pile on the carpet under the bed. There was an old hair net mixed with it, some burned matches, an unwrapped cake of 'hotel' soap, and on top of the pile was a note, printed the way a six-year-old child would do it, 'Evil spirit go away.'

"In the next few days we began looking through things in John's room and found lots of notes written in longhand, most of which were like those of a child just learning to write, although a few words were unmistakably John's handwriting. They were mainly of people's names, a date which might be the birthdate, and then another date some time in the future . . . some up past 1977. There were many names contained in the notes. One name was of a man I am sure John could not have known. He was Henry Anglin, a pitifully ignorant old man who used to farm just west of Grand Saline, and, like all farmers in the adjoining territory back in 1918, would come to town each Saturday to buy groceries and other supplies for the following week. When I was about fourteen years old I worked in a department store that also handled groceries. My job was to keep track of the farmers' stacks of groceries so that when they were ready to leave in the evening I could show them where their purchases were and help load their wagons. Henry Anglin was among the people I regularly waited on. He seemed old to me then and that was about fifty years ago. I have no doubt that he has long since died. I cannot imagine how his name entered John's mind. There were also some typewritten sheets in John's room which contained the same items as the notes we had found. One mentioned a certain 'Tink' Byford. There was a date that was probably his birthdate, then a date in 1964. We had moved to Tyler in July of 1964, and it was several months after that when I read in the paper that 'Tink' Byford had been killed in an auto accident while returning to Grand Saline from Dallas. Another name was 'Bill' Robertson, a friend of both of us. There was an early date, then 'Hosp. 1965, death 1967.' There were many other names, some now dead, but most still living, *always with two dates!* One day when I got home from work Andy and I found in the living room between the divan and table a new bar of soap which had been crumbled up and scattered over a two- or three-foot area. Andy found a potato masher in John's room with soap on it, so we assumed it was used in the living room where the soap was scattered. We did not clean it up right away. That night, after we went to bed, several pieces of soap about the size of a quarter hit our blinds like bullets, although the door to the living room was closed and the den and hallway are between the living room and our bedroom.

"I had had to wash some clothes that night, and it was after dark when I hung them on the line. While I was doing that, Andy came to the door and advised me that bugs and slugs were *flying* all over the house. I told him I thought I had heard something thud against the dog house near the clothesline. He checked and picked up a little leather wallet about the size of a billfold, which we had seen earlier in John's room, filled with loose tobacco. I told him to put it into the garbage can at the end of the house. The can had a lid on it. When I got through, it was time to take a bath and go to bed. While I was in the tub and Andy in the den, I heard something that sounded like a shotgun just outside the bathroom window. I called Andy to run out and see what he could find; he had heard the noise too. Just beneath the window he picked up the *same leather purse* he had put into the garbage can *an hour earlier!* It had hit the house flat, I suppose, near the bathroom window, to cause such a loud noise.

"During the preceding days we had found several other notes, all written or printed in the same peculiar way, as a little child might write. I had no idea what they meant, if anything, but some examples are:

Johnnie Beaird

1913 Murder
Bill Robertson—1967
The dog—leave 1965
Die 1972

Joe Bailey—1972
Reid Lesser—1966
Tink Byford—1964

Amy Beaird
The End

"In a little notebook we found:

Allie L. Lewis (This woman worked for the same company we did, and probably still does).
Luther Anderson (He owns a truck line that hauls salt).
Die 1980
Jeraldine Fail (This woman used to be a good friend of John's).
Die 1977
Louise Beaird (This is my sister, who would be 118 years of age in 2018).
Die 2018

"One day we found an old wooden box where John had kept her canceled checks. She had burned something in it, as the ashes were still in the box. The only thing left was one half of a calling card saying, 'burn spirit burn.' On just a scratch of paper were the words, 'Johnnie Beaird—Death 1991.'

"There were many more. Note the peculiar use of capital letters. All of these notes were printed:

<table>
<tr>
<td>JoHN is goIN
to Die</td>
<td>Be NIce IN
FROnt
OF
OLD FOOL-
ish MacK</td>
<td>There IS A
Hertz in Mt
PleaSant
SnEak
AWAY From
There (I
checked, and
there is not a
Hertz in Mt.
Pleasant).</td>
<td>I pOisOned
little FOOLS
white kittEn
ShALL i
poisOn The
Jap Cat (Andy
did have a
white kitten
which had
died for some
reason, and at
this time still
had a
Siamese cat).</td>
</tr>
</table>

"On a Canton bank blank check was written in the 'pay to' line: Johnnie B. Walker $1,000,000; in the 'for' line: Bill is NUTTY, and on the 'signature' line: ha ha.

"The ghastly events continued through October and into November, when they seemed to be letting up a little. One day early in the month when I got home from work Andy took me into John's room. Lined up under the edge of her bed but behind the spread were some pictures in little frames of various kinds. There was one of Amy, of John and Andy, of me, of Thelma Lowrie, who had been John's best friend and who had died in 1951, and several others. I don't know what significance they were supposed to have, but I left them right there. I assumed that John had been to the house that day. Bugs, dead and alive, continued to bombard us every night; even the slugs started flying through the air, smashing against the blinds and walls, making an awful mess wherever they hit.

"I decided to clean up both bedrooms as soon as I could, and to start by taking up the carpets. While I was doing that Andy found a note in John's room saying: 'Bugs will end for ThursDay Dec. 29.' I think the 23rd was the day I cleaned up our room, and the bugs were worse than ever that night, so we decided that maybe it was meant that the 23rd would be the last night. The next night, strangely enough, was pretty quiet.

"On the 24th I took up the carpet in John's room. While doing that I was hit by hundreds of bugs, slugs, and even some of the *nails I pulled out of the floor simply flew through the air and hit against the blinds.* Finally I was able to completely clean the room, paint the walls and woodwork, put up curtains, and the room looked very nice when I was finished.

"On November 26 I cleaned the house thoroughly, and no unusual activity took place that night. On the 27th bugs were everywhere. Just before dark I was taking a bath, and when I was through, standing up in the tub, I saw something hit the screen but could not tell what it was. I called

Andy from the den and told him to go out to see what it was. It turned out to be one of John's rubber gloves I had put out beside the garbage can to be hauled off.

"On Thanksgiving day I took all of our outside locks and had Andy take them to a locksmith in town the next morning to have them changed and get new keys, as I was convinced that John had been somehow coming from Daingerfield and using her keys to get in. I put the locks in place on Saturday. On Wednesday, December 1, 1965, somebody (I supposed it was John) punched a hole in the back screen door near the hook and unhooked the door. If it was John, though, her key would not fit.

"December 4 was the worst. It was Saturday, and we went to bed about 10:30. Something that sounded exactly like fingers drummed lightly on the bed. Although we were under the covers we could feel *whatever it was tugging at the sheets,* actually trying to jerk the covers off us! We would turn on the light and the tugging would stop. There were no bugs that night, but when the lights were off both Andy and I could feel something on our arms that seemed like small flying bugs bouncing up and down, sort of like gnats might do. We would slap at them, but there was absolutely nothing there. We would turn the lights on and see nothing. We sprayed the air everywhere with insect spray but it did no good. It felt exactly like someone lightly grabbing the hair on your arms with the thumb and forefinger, not actually pulling very hard at first, but later jerking the hair hard enough to hurt.

"While we were lying in bed with the light on, my shoes, weighing possibly two pounds each, *flew right over our heads* and landed on the other side of the bed. Andy's house shoes got up from the floor and flung themselves against the blinds. My clothes, which were hanging in the closet *with the door closed,* got out of there somehow *with-*

out the door being opened and landed across the room. Finally we turned off the lights and heard a strange sound we could not identify. It was under the bed, and sounded like bed rollers being turned rapidly with the fingers; but the bed was not even on rollers! Suddenly something hit the blind like a bullet. We turned on the light and found that the handle from the gas jet *under the bed had unscrewed itself, and both the bolt and the handle had flung themselves against the blind.* Then the bed started moving away from the wall. We would roll it back again only to have it do the same thing over and over. That was about all we could stand, and as it was 2 a.m. Sunday, I told Andy to put on his clothes. *We went to a motel to spend the rest of the night.*

"As we were walking down the driveway, after closing and locking the door, *a handkerchief still folded hit me on the back of the neck.* Just as we got in the car another handkerchief I had left on the bedside table hit me on the back after I had closed the car doors.

"We were so weary that we were asleep almost by the time we were in bed at the motel, and nothing happened to us while we were there. We came home about 9:30 the next morning. Some of John's clothes were in my closet, and most of mine were in hers. All sorts of weird notes were flying all about the house. I cleaned the house, and just as I was through, a *big cigar hit the back of my neck from out of nowhere.* I put it in the kitchen waste basket. Andy wanted some soup, so I started to a Cabell grocery store a few blocks away. Just as I left the house Andy saw the cigar jump up out of the waste basket and land on the floor. He put it back in the basket. When he came to the door to tell me about it I was getting into the car parked at the foot of the driveway, and when I turned toward him *I saw the cigar come sailing over his head and land at the side of the car,* about sixty feet from the house. When I came back and stepped in the door from the garage to the kitchen *I saw a clean shirt of mine come flying from the den* and land near the back door of the kitchen.

"By this time I had decided that it did absolutely no good to change the locks on the doors, although John had not broken in, if, indeed, this was John. Apparently whoever it was did not *need* a door, nor did he need to break in. Andy and I were standing in the kitchen watching things fly through the air, when all of a sudden his cap, which had been resting on the refrigerator, hit me in the back of the head. A roll of paper towels flew through the air; a can of soup on the cabinet top jumped off onto the floor several times after Andy picked it up and put it back.

"All of a sudden we heard a click. The toaster had been turned on, and the click meant it had turned itself off. *There was a piece of soap in it, melted!* A note nearby read 'clean toaster.' I felt something like a slight brush on my shoulder and heard Andy shout, 'Look out!' He saw the faint *outline of a hand which looked like his mother's* vanish near my head.

"Later, while in the den, I began to ask questions aloud, such as: 'John, tell me where we stayed last night?' A few seconds later a note came floating down in front of us, reading: 'Motel on T. B. Road. Couldn't get in.' 'Got to go, you've ruined me.' We did spend the night before at a motel on the road to the Tuberculosis Hospital where I work. I then said aloud, trying to sound funny in a totally unfunny situation: 'With all that power, why don't you just drop $5,000 on us?' Almost immediately a check with nothing but $5,000 written on the face dropped from out of nowhere. I said, 'John, why don't you appear here before us right this minute?' In about five seconds a note came down saying. 'Can't come ToDay haPPy YuLeTide.' I then asked, 'Are we going to be able to sleep tonight?' This answer came down to us: 'CaN't maKE aNyTHing haPPen tONighT you BROKE MY POWER Call HOUsTon.'

"Previously she told me to call Houston police and ask them about a witch who had solved the murder of a man named Gonzales. I felt like a fool, but I did call the Houston police department. I told them they could think I was drunk, crazy, or anything they wished to, but I just wanted a yes or no answer, and asked if they had any record of a witch ever helping the Houston police solve a murder of a man named Gonzales. The man I talked to did not appear surprised and simply asked me to wait a moment, and a few seconds later said that he could find no record of any such event.

"John had also given us directions for breaking her power. It was to 'break an egg, mix with a little water and a dash of salt and then throw it out in the back yard.'

"I have never been superstitious before, and this sounded awfully silly to me, but I think I would have done absolutely anything I was told if it meant a chance to put an end to these uncanny events, so I told Andy to go ahead and follow the directions. That night we had a few bugs and a note came floating down reading, 'power will end at 10 o'clock give or take an hour.'

"For several days we received what seemed like hundreds of *notes from right out of nowhere, simply materializing in midair, some folding themselves as they came toward us.* Some time after he had seen the hand vanish near my head, Andy was sitting in the den facing the outside windows. For a few fleeting seconds he saw the outline of John in front of the windows. Her back was to him as she looked out the windows, and Andy heard a faint 'goodbye' just as the figure melted in the air.

"We heard other voices after talking with John. All

seemed very strained, especially the female speakers, and they would often say that they had a 'mist' in their throat and could not continue talking to me, although they could always talk to Andy and he would hear them. I have dozens of notes that fell down to us from somewhere above, and most of them are from the same two people who stayed with us for the longest period of time. One of these was Mrs. Elliott who had been dead for three or four years when all this began to happen. The other was from a Mr. Gree, of whom I had never heard, but who seemed eager to help Andy and me with advice, especially concerning the care of Andy's cats and dogs. We were 'visited' by a great variety of 'people,' some long since dead, some still living, most of whom we know, or knew, but also some well-known public figures whose names were often in the news. I dated the notes from then on, but at times so many descended on us at once that I did not try to record the exact order in which we received them.

"It was Henry Anglin who tormented us from the very beginning, and who caused us to move out of the house. One night Anglin came to our room after we had gone to bed and his voice asked if he could cook himself an egg. We heard nothing else from him that night, but the next morning when I went to the kitchen to prepare breakfast, there in a teflon-lined skillet on the stove burner which was turned down low was an egg burned to a crisp!

"Another night Anglin came to our room and insisted that I call Houston. This was about the time he was beginning to be so terribly mean. I told him that I had already made one silly call to the Houston police, and that I had no intention of doing it again. He countered that I had not questioned them enough, and for me to phone them again. I refused, and he tormented us relentlessly. Finally he said he would leave us alone if we would drive around the loop, which was a distance of a little over twenty miles around the city of Tyler. Andy and I put on our clothes and did just that. We drove completely around the town, and sure enough, when we got home we were able to sleep the rest of the night without further trouble.

"A few nights after this, both Mrs. Elliott and Mrs. Snow told me verbally, while I was working in my shop, that they had taken Henry Anglin 'back to his grave,' and had driven a stake, prepared by Mr. Gree, through Anglin's heart. They promised that he would not bother us again.

"About this time we received notes allegedly from people who were still living, and also some from persons other than those previously mentioned who had been dead for several years. Among those still living were Mrs. W. H. Jarvis, and Odell Young, who lives in Grand Saline at this time. I also had one note from Mr. W. H. Quinn, *who had been dead for several years.* He used to be a railroad agent in Grand Saline. For a number of years I had occasion to have him sign numerous shipping papers, so I had become familiar with his handwriting. The note I got from him *was written in the same backhand fashion.* I believe that this note was written by him:

Dear Howard and Andy,

I pay tribute to you. You have put up with a lot from old man Anglin. It is all over now. Friday I am going to my grave to join my wife, whom I love. I am going to Marion's house to see him once more. He is my favorite child. I have always liked you, John and the boy and hope someday you will be together again.

Hiram Quinn

P.S. I enjoyed hearing about John going with Marion to get new teeth.

"The P. S. about his son's false teeth refers to the time about thirty years ago when John and I went to see Marion just after he had received his first set of dentures. At that time we lived just across the street from Marion and his wife and were friendly with them.

"We also got notes allegedly from Marilyn Monroe, Dorothy Kilgallen, and former Governor Jim Allred, who sympathized with us for what Henry Anglin was doing to us and about John's condition. Mrs. Snow and Mrs. Elliott had previously told us that Anglin had caused many deaths, some by auto accident, and some by switching a person's pills, *as they said he had done in the case of Dorothy Kilgallen.* The note we received with her name also said that was the cause of her death. I am not certain, but I believe they also said Anglin caused Marilyn Monroe's death.

"None of the people still living, except John, ever spoke to me; they just dropped their notes from the air. Mrs. Jarvis actually spoke to Andy, though, and had him tell me to answer aloud each of the questions she put in her note to me. Mr. Quinn's note was stuck in the grate between the kitchen and my shop.

"For the first few weeks in January 1966 only Mrs. Elliott and Mr. Jack Gree 'visited' us. She and I had lots of conversations, but she gradually got so she could barely talk to me, although Andy could still hear her. The notes were written either on some note paper Andy kept in the kitchen or on some Canton, Texas, bank deposit slips in John's room. If I was working in my shop she would stick the notes in the grill and bang on the wall to attract my attention, and then I would stoop down under the work bench and retrieve the note. Mr. Gree, who told us we had never heard of him, had a very low, deep, gruff voice. Most of his communications to me were in the form of notes, however, but he and Andy carried on lengthy conversations nearly every day. He also used the grill 'post office' for depositing his notes, then banged on the wall to let me know they were there.

"At times, when Andy and I were in the car, Mrs. Elliott or Mr. Gree would be with us. They would ride along for a while and then suddenly say they were going to Canada, Russia, Minnesota, or some other far-off place, saying it took only two or three minutes for them to travel those distances, and then we might not hear anything else from them until the next day or night. Early in January of 1966 Andy came out to my shop and said Mr. Gree wanted to know if it was OK for him to use the telephone, and of course I told him it was. I did not know what control I would have had over the situation anyway. That first time he said it was something personal and asked Andy if he would mind leaving the room. *I could hear the phone being dialed,* and stooped down near the floor so I could look through the grilled opening, but of course I could not see anyone there and could not quite see the phone itself. After that he used the phone many times, while I was working and while Andy was studying at the kitchen table in full view of the telephone. *It was really spooky to see the receiver stand up on end by itself, and then after a while put itself back down where it belonged,* but always upside down. Some nights he would dial many times after we had gone to bed, and we could hear the sound plainly in our bedroom. The next morning I would find the receiver on the phone upside down. One night while Andy was taking a bath Mr. Gree called somebody *and I heard him say* in a low, deep voice, 'I'm weird . . . I'm unusual.' I thought to myself, 'You can say that again.' He repeated it several times and then all I could hear would be a series of low grunts, from which I could not make out any real words. One evening while we were in the car coming home from the post office I asked Andy whom he supposed Mr. Gree called on the phone. Without a moment's hesitation Mrs. Elliott, who we did not know was with us, spoke up and said he was calling her. We did not ask her where she was when she received the call!

"Both Mr. Gree and Mrs. Elliott certainly had Andy's welfare in mind. Practically every day for the whole month of January there was a note from one of them stuck in the screen door. It appeared to be Mrs. Elliott's job to help get John home and to take care of Andy. She said if she could do that she would probably go back to her grave early.

"After John had left home I felt very sorry for Andy. He was lonely being at home alone so much of the time. He indicated a desire for a cat, and a little later for a dog. At the insistence and complete direction of Mrs. Elliott I spent quite a sum of money for such pets. Mr. Gree then took over completely the directions for our taking care of these dogs and cats.

"On January 29, 1966, while I was writing a letter, there was a pounding on the kitchen wall, indicating that there was a note in our 'post office.' It was from Mrs. Elliott. 'I love that beagle. Sorry the dogs have been sick. I feel responsible. Andy worries. He loves them so much. If something happens to one don't let it worry you. Andy understands that one dog is a good companion and easier. If something does happen I only hope it isn't the beagle. The beagle will be a better companion. Andy would give up one if you asked him to. Not that he wants to. But he would understand. He loves dogs. He understands. El. Reply to this note. Reply to every line I wrote.'

"The other dog she referred to was a brown dachshund, which did not look very healthy when we bought it. It never did gain any weight and after we had given away the black dachshund the brown one continued to get worse.

During the next few days and nights some of the most unbelievable things happened in connection with this brown dachshund. I would be working in my shop and suddenly hear a slight noise on the roof of the house. It would be utterly impossible for the dog to jump up there from the ground, and there was nothing else around for him to get on in order to jump up on the house. *Yet there he was clear up on the peak walking from one end to the other!* We would get a ladder and finally coax him down into the eave where we could get hold of him and put him on the ground. This happened time after time. We finally decided to leave him up there and go on to bed. The next night Mrs. Elliott told us she knew about the dog. We asked her how it was possible and said we would like to see how the dog got up there. She said we could not see it . . . that it was just a case of 'now he's down here . . . now he's up there.' She said that even if we were watching him, he would just simply vanish from his spot on the ground and at the same instant be on the roof. Later that night Mrs. Elliott called Andy and me and said the dog was trying to commit suicide and for us to go to the back door and look in the flower bed on the south side of the back steps. Sure enough we looked, and the ground had been freshly dug and looked as if it had been loosely put back in place. We could see the dirt moving, and I told Andy to go and get the shovel from the garage. Mrs. Elliott said it was not in the garage, but for us to wait just a few seconds and we would find it out in the front yard under the tree, where it would be when it got back from 'Heaven.' Andy did go and found the shovel just where she said it would be and brought it to me. I dug down beside where the dirt was moving and pulled the dog out by his tail. He was barely breathing and looked very pitiful, but after a few seconds was able to feebly walk a little. Mrs. Elliott told us that we had better put it out of its misery that night. I told her I did not have anything to put it to sleep with, but she finally told me to just go ahead and kill it, using a hammer, a brick or anything that would put it to death. It was a sickening experience, but I did kill the dog with a brick, as I was certain that it was in pain and would be better off dead. *We buried the dog where it had apparently dug its own grave!* I cannot say that the dog actually dug this hole, crawled into it and covered itself up with dirt, as I find it hard to see how it could possibly have dragged the dirt in on top of it . . . I have only Mrs. Elliott's word for that. I am merely stating what she told us, although I did find the dog in the hole, covered with loose dirt, and barely breathing when I pulled it out.

"While John was away in Daingerfield, I had bought a little plastic toilet bowl cleaner on which a disposable pad is used. The handle had come apart the first time I tried to use it. It cost only a few cents, and ordinarily I would have just bought another and forgotten about it. However, I decided to write the manufacturer, and some time later I received a letter from them, advising me that they were sending me another handle. Eventually I received a notice that there was a package at the post office. I would have had to drive about ten miles from the place where I work to the post office and back during the noon hour to pick it up, and since it was of no importance I intended to just wait until Saturday to call for the package. That evening, though, when I went to my shop to start work there was a package on my work bench. The shop had been locked all day and was still locked when I started to work. I asked Andy if he knew anything about it and he assured me that he did not even know about the package being in the post office. At that moment Mrs. Elliott spoke up and admitted she had gotten it out of the post office and brought it home to me!

"Not long after John had gone to Daingerfield another mystifying thing happened. In one of the kitchen drawers where we kept some silverware in one of those little compartments made for that purpose, there was a space five or six inches behind that section clear across the drawer. In there I kept a few tools such as a screwdriver, pliers, tack hammer, where they would be conveniently available when I needed them. I had not had occasion to look in there for some time, and when I finally did I noticed a pistol. It was a .22 cal. and looked very real, and only when I picked it up did I discover that it was just a blank pistol. I asked Andy where it came from, but he knew nothing whatever about it. Mrs. Elliott spoke up and said *she* had brought it from Daingerfield. She told us that John had ordered it from some magazine ad and had paid $12 for it. She said it was awfully hard for her to bring it to our house and that it had taken her several hours to do so. She did not say why she did it but intimated that she just wanted us to know about it. Later, when we were moving away from that house, the pistol was gone, and I have not seen it since.

"For many years I had owned a .25 cal. Colt automatic pistol. I always kept it in good condition but it had not been fired in thirty years at the time we moved to Tyler. John's mother also had had a pistol exactly like mine except for the handles, as I bought a pair of white, carved bone handles for mine. When she died we brought that pistol to our house, although we never had occasion to shoot it either. We still had them both when we moved to Tyler. With so many mysterious events taking place, I decided to keep a pistol out in my shop, so I brought the one that had belonged to John's mother and left it on top of my work bench. It stayed there for several weeks. One night it was missing. My shop was always locked and I had the only key. I had wrapped my own gun in a polyethylene bag after cleaning it thoroughly, and put it in a little compartment between the two drawers in a chest in my room. One of the drawers had to be removed completely to get the gun, and even then one had to look closely to find it. I had told no one about the hiding place. When the gun in my shop suddenly disappeared I decided to get mine that I had hidden in the chest. However, when I looked in the hiding place my pistol was not there, *but in its place was the one which had been in my shop!* I did not take it to my shop then, but some time later when I did decide to, that gun too was gone, and we have seen neither of them since that time.

"Occasionally during all this time I would write to John, saying that I wished she would come home so that we might be able to get her well and be happy together again. She never replied to any of my letters, although she wrote Andy a note now and then when he would write her first. I talked to her on the phone a short while later. I do not remember whether I called her on the phone or whether she was the one who called, but she finally said she would be home on a given date in February 1967, and that Mack would bring her. When she got to Tyler she called me at work. She had taken a room in a private home for a few days before coming back to our house. Andy and I talked her into coming home that night, though, and during the remainder of 1967 things seemed to be more normal for us than they had been in many years.

"During March of 1967 I moved my shop to a building downtown. I was getting too crowded in the little room I had been using at the house, and when I got things all set up at the new location I thought that it would be good for John to run the shop during the day, or at least part of each day, which she agreed to do. Things went along very well throughout the rest of the year. Our daughter Amy came for a few days' visit at Christmastime. A little while before this, though, John had begun to throw cigarettes all over the house again, and there were burned places everywhere. John, of course, insisted that she had *not* thrown them there.

"Some time in late 1967 Mrs. Elliot reappeared and began giving us more advice about how to handle John. By this time I believe Andy was about to go to pieces. One of the officials of the school Andy attended called me and asked why Andy had not been to school. Mrs. Elliott had said for him not to go to school any more, that he could take a correspondence course and get his high school diploma that way. I tried to convince him to return to school.

"I received all sorts of notes from Mrs. Elliott, telling me that Andy was becoming a nervous wreck, and that if I tried to make him go back to school she would take him with her. Andy also told me he would rather go with *her* than to return to school. Finally I asked her why she did not get away from us and never return. The last note I received from her read as follows:

Howard,
You might wish I wouldn't come back but I did. You can do whatever you want to with John. I won't ask Jr. if he wants to come with me, though he might kill himself. Taking John away will only make him worry more. You don't care. THERE IS ONE THING YOU CARE ABOUT AND THAT IS YOU. I wish you would leave Jr. alone. He can get a course to finish school and get a diploma and leave you. If you cause any trouble I'll take him or he'll kill himself. I could help him go to California but that wouldn't be good he be better off dead, which he probably will be. There's not going to be a world in 15 years so he doesn't care. He just wants to have some enjoyment. You are real silly. John's going to get violent. That's the silliest thing I ever heard. Now you are really going to hurt things when you send John away. All I asked was 1 week. You don't want John well you

just want rid of her, so you cause trouble and get her mad. John doesn't cost you all that much money you selfish fool. I can't make John love you but I could get her to clean house and if you had any sense (which you don't) you would leave her at Trumark. Now when you send her away and start giving Jr. trouble you are going to be sorrier than you have been or will ever be. I don't know Jr. is good at music and would be excellent and be able to make 3 times your money. Maybe he will be better off gone. You silly old selfish idiot.

You can holler and anything else but it will be of no avail. When you see the nut doctor, tell him about me, maybe they'll put you away.

"During the last part of March and early February the most ghastly things yet began to happen at the house. Henry Anglin came back. I could not hear him, but Andy said he talked very little and what few words he did speak were barely understandable. Andy could hear his evil laughter. He began by putting an egg under the mattress about where my head would be. We would not have known at the time, of course, but he would tell Andy to have me look in certain places. There was an egg, broken, in one of my house shoes, one in a pocket of my robe, one in the shade of the ceiling light, one broken in the corner of the room where it was running down the wall, and one broken against the chest of drawers. There was even one inside my pillow case. Andy said that Anglin would just give a sort of insane-sounding laugh each time we would find another egg. We cleaned up the mess, and that was the end of the egg episode.

"A few days later when I got home from work, Andy called me into our room and there *in the middle of the bed was our dresser*. It was not very heavy, and I was able to lift it down by myself. The next day the chest of drawers was on the bed. This was very heavy, and it took both Andy and me to set it on the floor again. The following day,

when I got home, Andy was not there. I noticed that the door to the room he and I shared was closed. That was not unusual, though, as we often kept it closed during the day. However, when I started to open it, *it simply came off the hinges in my hands.* I could see that the pins had been removed from the hinges, so I just leaned the door against the wall. The next day I found the closet door wrenched from the opening, bringing most of the door facing with it. These were hollow doors and both of them had holes knocked in them about the size of a fist. The next night, about nine o'clock, while I was working at the shop, Andy telephoned me and said *the refrigerator was in our room.* He had heard a noise while he and John were watching television, and got up to see what it was. To reach the bedroom the refrigerator had had to go through the length of the breakfast room, the den, and a hallway before reaching our room. I knew we could not move it back that night so I told Andy to just leave it alone and we would decide what to do the next day. However, a little later he called and said the washing machine, which was located in the kitchen, had been pulled away from the wall and the faucets behind it were leaking and water was running all over the floor.

"I told him to cut off the hydrants which he did. I then called the police and asked them to meet me at the house. When we got there the holes in the two doors in the bedroom had *increased to about fifteen or twenty* and some of them were through both sides of the doors and big enough to put one's head through.

"Pretty soon, the house was swarming with policemen and detectives. That is when I decided to tell them as briefly as I could what we had been going through. Some of them, I am certain, thought the whole thing was a hoax, and came right out and said they thought I was being hoodwinked by John, who had enlisted Andy's help. That was absolutely ridiculous, though, *as practically all of the strange happenings occurred while Andy and I were together, and while John was staying with Mack about a hundred miles away.* One of the chief detectives talked a long time with John, and later told me that she talked sensibly, but that he was amazed at *her lack of concern about the strange things* that had happened. I too had noticed that she was wholly indifferent to the entire 'show.'

"About the middle of February 1968 things got so bad that I made John give me her key to the shop, and told her that I was going to have to do one of three things. I was going to try and have her committed to a state hospital as I was not financially able to have her take psychiatric treatments, or she could take them and pay for them herself, or I was going to get a divorce. A divorce at my age I thought was ridiculous, but I felt as if I could not stand to go on as things were. Andy was going to move with me as soon as I found a suitable place. John did not seem perturbed one way or the other, and probably did not believe I would really do any of those things. However, on February 24, I did move out of the house, and had my attorney begin divorce proceedings, since he again stated that he did not think I would have a chance in trying to have her committed. I think that when the papers were served on John it was the first time she actually realized what was happening. I got an apartment only a few blocks from my shop. I told Andy to call me every night to let me know how things were at home. I met him at a nearby shopping center each Saturday and gave him enough money to buy food for himself and John during the following week.

"For several weeks we went on this way. One night Andy

called me and said *that the dining table was up in the attic.* The only opening to the attic was a rectangular hole in the garage ceiling about 16 by 24 inches, through which *it was absolutely impossible for the table to go.* The next night the table was back in the house again. This happened several times. Other things also 'went' to the attic, such as a small table, an ottoman and another kidney-shaped end table. Finally, the dining table came down and Andy found it in the garage, and after considerable work was able to get it inside the house, where it belonged.

"Eventually, John was beginning to believe that the strange things we had been talking about were really happening. Previously she had just made fun of us whenever we would mention them. Several weeks after I had left, Andy was sitting in the den, playing his guitar, when the lights went out. At first he thought that a bulb had burned out, but when he looked at the switch he could see that it had *been turned off.* This happened several times. Once when John was going through the den the light went out and she too saw that the switch had been turned; Andy was not anywhere near it, and there was nobody else who could have done it.

"It was well into the second month after I left home. I had just finished work in the shop. The telephone rang. It was John and she sounded almost hysterical. She said she was very sick and begged me to come home. I got there a few minutes later, and she could hardly talk. She continued to beg me to come home, but I told her I could never spend another night in that house. Finally I got her calmed down enough to talk seriously. I finally told her that I would come back, but that first we would have to find another place to live. I demanded that she never smoke again. Finally, on April 15, 1968, we moved out of the house of horrors, and I have not been there since.

"John has not smoked since that time. It has now been over three months since we left the house, and John does the normal things about the house except cook. She is again at my rubber stamp shop and seems to enjoy it."

In retrospect, as I read over these words, I realized how difficult it must have been for Mr. Beaird to report on his experiences, especially to a stranger. What had appeared completely impossible to him would, of course, have been even more unbelievable to someone who was not present when it happened, and he doubted his own sanity at times, which was not surprising.

Having met Howard Beaird I am sure that he is completely sane, in fact, so sane he could not even be called neurotic. Had I not heard of parallel cases before, perhaps I too would have wondered about it. None of the phenomena reported by Mr. Beaird are, however, impossible in the light of parapsychological research. We are dealing here with forces that seem to be in contradiction of ordinary or orthodox physical laws, but the more we learn of the nature of matter and the structure of the atom the more it seems likely that poltergeist activities connect with physics in such a way as to make seeming de-materialization and re-materialization of solid objects possible practically without time loss. But the case was a question of studying not so much the techniques involved in the phenomena as the reasons behind them and those causing them.

I informed Mr. Beaird that I was eager to enter the case, especially as I wanted to make sure that the poltergeist activities had really ceased once and for all and would never recur at his new location. In cases of this kind there is always the possibility that the phenomena are attached to one or the other person in the household rather than to a location. Moving to another house seems to have stopped the activities, but as there had been pauses before that culminated in renewed and even stronger physical activities, I wanted to be sure that this would not be the case in this new location. I explained that I would have to interview all those concerned, even the police detectives who had come to the house on that fateful night. Mr. Beaird assured me that he would make all the necessary arrangements, and, after discussing my plans with his wife and son, they too agreed to talk to me. Mack, her sister-in-law, who had been hostess to Mrs. Beaird while most of the phenomena took place at the house, was unable to meet me in Tyler, but I was assured that Mrs. Beaird had never left her care during all that time. For a while Howard Beaird had thought that his wife had returned without his knowledge and done some of the things about the house that had startled him. This, of course, turned out to be a false impression. At no time did Mrs. Beaird leave her sister-in-law's house in Daingerfield, 75 miles away. Whether or not her astral self visited the home is another matter and would be subject to my investigation and verification as far as possible.

Mr. Beaird also went back to his former home to talk to the present owners. Somewhat suspicious of him, for no apparent reason, they were willing to see me if I came to Tyler. Mr. M. works for a local bakery and returns home at 5:30 p.m., and since his wife would not entertain strange visitors in the absence of her husband, my visit would have to be at such an hour as was convenient to the M.'s. Perhaps the somewhat battered condition of the house when the M.'s had bought it from Mr. Beaird might be the reason for their reluctance to discuss my visit. At any rate it was agreed that I could call briefly on them and talk to them about the matter at hand. Howard Beaird's daughter, who is now Mrs. Howard Wilson, lives in Austin, Texas. She has had some interest in the occult and mind development and had suggested that someone from the Silva Mind Center in Laredo should come up to Tyler to investigate the case. That was prior to my entering the situation, however, and now Mrs. Wilson wanted very much to come up to Tyler herself and be present during my investigation. Unfortunately it turned out later that she was unable to keep the date due to prior commitments. Thorough man that he is, Howard Beaird also talked to Detective Weaver at the police station to make sure I could see him and question him about his own investigation of the house. I was assured of the welcome mat at the police station, so I decided to set the time when I could go down to Tyler and look for myself into what appeared to be one of the most unusual cases of psychic phenomena.

On February 5, 1969, I arrived at the Tyler airport. It was 5:42 in the afternoon and Howard Beaird was there to welcome me. We had made exact plans beforehand so he whisked me away to the Blackstone Hotel, allowed me to check in quickly, then went on with me to see Detective Weaver at the police station.

As we passed through town I had the opportunity to observe what Tyler, Texas, was all about. Clean shops, quiet streets, a few tree-lined avenues, small houses, many of them very old—well, old anyway in terms of the United States—and people quietly going about their business seem to be characteristic of this small town. We passed by Howard Beaird's shop, a neat, tidy little shop, the company name Trumark plainly written on the window pane. As in many small towns the telephone wires were all above ground, strung in a lazy haphazard fashion from street to street. The police station turned out to be a modern concrete building set back a little from the street. Detective

Weaver readily agreed to talk to me. Howard Beaird left us for the moment in a fine sense of propriety just in case the detective wanted to say something not destined for his ears. As it turned out there wasn't anything he could not have said in front of him. Was there anything in the detective's opinion indicating participation by either the boy or Mrs. Beaird in the strange phenomena? The detective shrugged. There was nothing he could pinpoint along these lines. He then went to the files and extricated a manila envelope inscribed "pictures and letter, reference mysterious call at——— Elizabeth, February 19, 1968, 11:00 p.m., case number 67273. Officer B. Rosenstein and officer M. Garrett." Inside the envelope there were two pictures, photographs taken at the time by a police photographer named George Bain. One picture was of the door, clearly showing the extreme violence with which a hole had been punched into it. The entire rim of the hole was splintered as if extremely strong methods had been employed to punch this hole through the door.

The other picture showed a heavy chest of drawers of dark wood sitting squarely upon a bed. Quite clearly the description given to me by Howard Beaird had been correct. What exactly did the two police officers find when they arrived at the house on Elizabeth Street? The house was in disorder, the detective explained, and furniture in places where it wasn't supposed to be. On the whole he bore out the description of events given by Howard Beaird.

Somehow he made me understand that the police did not accept the supernatural origin of the phenomena even though they could not come up with anything better in the way of a solution. Almost reluctantly, the officer wondered whether perhaps Andy wasn't in some way responsible for the phenomena although he did not say so in direct words. I decided to discuss the practical theories concerning poltergeists with him and found him amazingly interested. "Would you like to have the photographs?" the detective asked and handed me the folder. Surprised by his generosity, I took the folder and I still have it in my files. It isn't very often that a researcher such as I is given the original folder from the files of a police department. But then the mystery on Elizabeth Street is no longer an active situation—or is it?

After we had thanked Detective Weaver for his courtesies we decided to pay a visit to the house itself. After a moment of hesitation, the officer suggested that he come along since it might make things easier for us. How right he was. When we arrived at the house on Elizabeth Street and cautiously approached the entrance, with me staying behind at first, there was something less than a cordial reception awaiting us. Mr. M. was fully aware of my purpose, of course, so that we were hardly surprising him with all this.

After a moment of low-key discussion at the door between Howard Beaird and Detective Weaver on one hand and Mr. M. on the other, I was permitted to enter the house and look around for myself. The M. family had come to see me, if not to greet me, and looked at me with curious eyes. I explained politely and briefly that I wanted to take some photographs for the record and I was permitted to do so. I took black and white pictures with a high sensitivity film in various areas of the house, especially the kitchen area where it connects with the garage and the living room, both places where many of the phenomena have been reported in Mr. Beaird's testimony.

On developing these, under laboratory conditions, we found there was nothing unusual except perhaps certain bright light formations in the kitchen area where there should be none since no reflective surfaces existed. Then

I returned to the living room to talk briefly with Mr. M. and his family.

Was there anything unusual about the house that he had noticed since he had moved in? Almost too fast he replied, "Nothing whatsoever. Everything was just fine." When Mr. M. explained how splendid things were with the house he shot an anxious look at his wife, and I had the distinct impression they were trying to be as pleasant and as superficial as possible and to get rid of me as fast as possible. Did they have any interest in occult phenomena such as ghosts? I finally asked. Mr. M. shook his head. Their religion did not allow them such considerations, he explained somewhat sternly. Then I knew the time had come to make my departure.

I made inquiries with real estate people in the area and discovered a few things about the house neither Mr. Beaird nor Mr. M. had told me. The house was thirteen years old and had been built by a certain Terry Graham. There had been two tenants before the Beairds. Prior to 1835 the area had been Indian territory and was used as a cow pasture by the Cherokee Indians.

I also discovered that Mrs. M. had complained to the authorities about footsteps in the house when there was no one walking, of doors opening by themselves, and the uncanny feeling of being watched by someone she could not see. That was shortly after the M.'s had moved into the house. The M.'s also have young children. It is conceivable that the entities who caused such problems to the Beaird family might have been able to manifest through them also. Be this as it may, the matter was not followed up. Perhaps their religious upbringing and beliefs did not permit them to discuss such matters and they preferred to ignore them, or perhaps the activities died of their own volition. At any rate, it seemed pretty certain to me that the poltergeist activities did not entirely cease with the removal of the Beairds from the house. But did these activities continue in the new house the Beairds had chosen for their own? That was a far more important question.

I asked Howard Beaird to send me a report of further activities if and when they occurred at the new house. On February 23 he communicated with me by letter. I had asked him to send me samples of John's and Andy's handwriting so that I could compare them with the notes he had let me have for further study. In order to arrive at a satisfactory explanation of the phenomena it was, of course, necessary to consider all ordinary sources for them. Amongst the explanations one would have to take into account was the possibility of either conscious or unconscious fraud, that is to say, the writing of the notes by either John or Andy and their somehow manipulating them so that they would seem to appear out of nowhere in front of Mr. Beaird. For that purpose I needed examples of the two handwritings to compare them with some of the handwritings on the notes.

There were a number of noises in the new home that could be attributed to natural causes. But there were two separate incidents which, in the opinion of Howard Beaird, could not be so explained. Shortly before I arrived in Tyler a minor incident occurred which makes Howard wonder whether the entities from beyond the veil are still with him in the new house. One evening he had peeled two hard-boiled eggs in order to have them for lunch the following day. He had placed them in the refrigerator on a paper towel. The following morning he discovered that both eggs were frozen solid even though they were still on the lower shelf of the refrigerator. This could only have been accomplished if they had spent considerable time in the freezer compartment during the night. Questioning his wife and son as to whether they had put the eggs in the freezer, he discovered that neither of them had done so. He decided to test the occurrence by repeating the process. He found that the two new eggs which he had placed in the refrigerator that night were still only chilled but not frozen the next day. What had made the first pair of eggs as hard as stone he is unable to understand, but he is satisfied that the occurrence may be of non-psychic origin.

Then there was the matter of a clock playing a certain tune as part of its alarm clock device. Through no apparent reason this clock went off several times, even though no one had been near it. Even though it had not been wound for a long time and had only a 24-hour movement, it played this tune several times from deep inside a chest of drawers. Eventually the clock was removed, and in retrospect Mr. Beaird does not think that a supernatural situation could have been responsible for it. But the two separate incidents did frighten the Beairds somewhat. They were afraid that the change of address had not been sufficient to free them from the influences of the past. As it turned out, the move was successful and the separation complete.

I had to work with two kinds of evidence. There was, first of all, the massive evidence of mysterious notes which had fallen out of the sky and which showed handwriting of various kinds. Perhaps I could make something out of that by comparing them with the handwritings of living people. Then there was the question of talking personally and in depth with the main participants, the Beairds, and, finally, to see what others who knew them had to say about them. Howard Beaird's daughter, Amy, now Mrs. Howard C. Wilson, thought that the real victim of what she thought "a circus of horrors" was her brother Andy. "If you had known Andy when he was small, up to the time mother began to show real signs of her illness, it would be impossible for you to recognize him as the same person now. He was typically, for a little boy, simply brimming over with mischievous humor. He would do anything to make people laugh and would run simply hooting with joy through the house when he had done something devilish." That was not the Andy I met when I came to Tyler. The boy I talked to was quiet, withdrawn, painfully shy, and showed definite signs of being disturbed.

The following morning I went to see the Beairds at their new home. The home itself is pleasant and small and stands in a quiet, tree-lined street. As prearranged, Mr. Beaird left me alone with each of the two other members of his family so that I could speak to them in complete confidence. Andy, a lanky boy, seemed ill at ease at first when we sat down. In order to gain his confidence, I talked about songs and the records popular at the time, since I had seen a number of record albums in his room. Somehow this helped open him up; he spoke more freely after that. Now sixteen, he was studying at a local barber college. When I wondered how a young man, in this day and age, would choose this somewhat unusual profession, he assured me that the money was good in this line of work and that he really liked it. He felt he could put his heart and soul into it. After some discussion of the future as far as Andy was concerned, I brought the conversation around to the matter at hand.

"When these peculiar events took place you and your father lived alone in the other house. Did you ever see anyone?" "Well, I had seen a vision of my mother this one time. It looked like her but nobody was there really . . . kind of like a shadow, or a form." "Have you seen the notes?" "Yes." "Did you ever actually see anyone writing them?" "No." "Did you ever hear any voices?" "Yeh. I talked to them." "How did they sound?" "Well, the women that were here all sounded alike . . . real high voices. The men were dead, you know . . . the spirits, or whatever you want to call them. They had real deep voices. They were hard to understand." "Did they talk to you in the room?" "From out of nowhere. No matter where I might be." "You didn't see them anywhere?" "Never saw them." "Was your father with you at the time you heard the voices or were you alone?" "He was with me at times and not at others." "These voices . . . are they in the daytime or are they at night?" "At night . . . mostly at night, or afternoon, when I'd get home from school." "Did it start right after you moved in?" "No . . . it was two or three months after . . . " "Did you see the insects?" "Oh yes." "Where did they come from?" "It seemed like just out of the ceiling." "Could they have come in any other way?" "They couldn't have come in . . . not that many." "Whose voices did you hear?" "First of all my mother's." "The time she was away at Daingerfield?" "Yes." "What did the voice sound like?" "The same high voice. It sounded a little like her." "What did she say?" "She started to talk about my grandfather's funeral and about someone being mean to her."

Clearly the boy was not at his best. Whether it was my presence and the pressure the questioning was putting on him or whether he genuinely did not remember, he was somewhat uncertain about a lot of the things his father had told me about. But he was quite sure that he had heard his mother's voice at a time when she was away at Daingerfield. He was equally sure that none of the insects could have gotten into the house by ordinary means and that the notes came down, somehow of their own volition, from the ceiling. I did not wish to frighten him and thanked him for his testimony, short though it was. I then asked that John, Mrs. Beaird that is, be asked to join me in the front room so we could talk quietly. Mrs. Beaird seemed quite at ease with me and belied the rather turbulent history I knew she had had. Evidently the stay at her sister-in-law's house and the prior psychiatric treatment had done some good. Her behavior was not at all unusual; in fact, it was deceivingly normal. Having seen one of her earlier photographs I realized that she had aged tremendously. Of course I realized that her husband would have discussed many of the things with her so that she would have gained secondhand knowledge of the phenomena. Nevertheless, I felt it important to probe into them because sometimes a person thinks she is covering up while, in fact, she is giving evidence.

"Now we are going to discuss the other house," I said pleasantly. "Do you remember some of the events that happened in the other house?" "Well, I wasn't there when they took place. They told me about it . . . and actually, you will learn more from my son than from me because I don't know anything." "You were away all that time?" "Yes." "Before you went, did anything unusual happen?" "Nothing." "After you came back did anything happen?" "Well, I don't know . . . I don't remember anything." "Before you bought the house, did you ever have any unusual experience involving extrasensory perception at any time?" "Never. I know nothing whatever about it." "You were living somewhere else for a while." "I was with my sister-in-law." "How would you describe that period of your life? Was it an unhappy one? A confusing one? What would you say that period was?" "I have never been unhappy. I have never been confused." "Why did you go?" "I felt I needed to for personal reasons." "During that time did you have contact with your husband and son? Did you telephone or did you come back from time to time?" "I did not come back, but I had some letters from them and I believe that I talked some . . . " "Did your husband ever tell you some of the things that had happened in your absence?" "Yes. He told me." "What did you make of it?" "I didn't understand it. If I had seen it, I'd have gotten to the bottom of it somehow." "The people who are mentioned in some of these notes, are you familiar with them? Were there any of them that you had a personal difficulty with or grudge against?" "None whatever. They were friends." "Now, you are familiar with this lady, Mrs. Elliott, who has, apparently, sent some notes." "Oh yes. She was a very good friend of mine. Of course, she is much older. She had a daughter my age and we were very good friends." "Did you have any difficulties?" "I have no difficulties," she replied and her eyes filled with tears. "No? You had at the time you left here." "Not real difficulties. For several reasons, I needed a change. I didn't intend to stay so long. She was living alone and she worked during the day. And we sort of got into a most enjoyable relationship whereby I took care of certain household chores while she was gone . . . " "What made you stay so long?" "I just really can't tell you what it was." "You still have no answer to the puzzle as to what happened?" "None. I have no idea." "Do you remember having any treatments?" "I'm just getting old. That is the difficulty."

It was clear that her mind had blocked out all memory of the unpleasant occurrences in her life. As often happens with people who have undergone psychiatric treatment, there remains a void afterwards, even if electric shock therapy has not been used. Partially this is, of course, due to the treatment, but sometimes it is self-induced deliberately by the patient in order to avoid discussing the unpleasant. Mrs. Beaird had returned to her husband and son to resume life and try to make the best of it. To go back over the past would have served no purpose from her point of view. This was not a matter of refusing to discuss these things with me. She did not remember them quite consciously and no amount of probing would have helped, except perhaps in-depth hypnosis, and I was not prepared to undertake this with a former mental patient. Clearly then I could not get any additional material from the principal. I decided to re-examine the evidence and talk again with the one man who seemed, after all, the most reliable witness in the entire case, Mr. Beaird himself.

In particular, I wanted to re-examine his own personal observations of certain phenomena, for it is one thing to make a report alone, quietly, filled with the memory of what one has experienced, and another to report on phenomena while being interrogated by a knowledgeable, experienced investigator. Quite possibly some new aspects might be unearthed in this fashion. At the very least it would solidify some of the incredible things that had happened in the Beaird household.

On the morning of February 6, 1969, I met with Howard Beaird at my hotel and we sat down, quietly, to go over the fantastic events of the past three years. In order to arrive at some sort of conclusion, which I wanted very much to do, I had to be sure that Mr. Beaird's powers of observation had been completely reliable. In going over some of his statements once again I wasn't trying to be repetitive but rather to observe his reaction to my questions and to better determine in my own mind whether or not he had observed correctly. In retrospect I can only say that Howard Beaird was completely unshaken and repeated, in essence, exactly what he had reported to me earlier. I feel that he has been telling the truth all along, neither embellishing it nor diminishing it. Our conversation started on a calm unemotional note which was now much more possible than at the time when he first made his report to me, when he was still under the influence of recent events. Things had been quiet at the house and seemed to continue to remain quiet, so he was able to gather his thoughts more clearly and speak of the past without that emotional involvement which would have made it somewhat more difficult for me to judge his veracity.

"Now we had better start at the beginning. I am interested in discussing whatever *you yourself* observed. Your wife was still in the house when the first thing happened?" "Yes." "Were those *real* bugs?" "Yes." "When you turned the light on?" "You could see thousands of bugs on the floor." "How did you get rid of them?" "We had a vacuum cleaner." "Did they come from the direction of the windows or the door?" "The door." "Now, after the bugs, what was the next thing that you personally observed?" "I heard my wife's voice. After my son and I had gone to bed we were lying there talking about these things that had happened. That was after she had left Tyler." "Did it sound like her voice?" "No. It didn't sound like her voice to me but it was *her* . . . " "Well, how did you know it was her?" "She told me it was and was talking about my sister having insulted her. Nobody else knew that except my wife and I." "Where did the voice seem to come from? Was it in the room?" "Yes." "What happened after that?" "Several nights after that, she appeared to Andy. I heard him talking in the bathroom. He talked for two or three minutes and then I heard him say, well, goodbye." "Didn't it make you feel peculiar? His mother was obviously not there and he was talking to her?" "Well, I had already had my encounter with her." "Did you call your wife in Daingerfield?" "No." "Why not?" "Well, she wouldn't have believed me. I had thought about writing her sister-in-law and telling her that you've got to keep my wife in Daingerfield. I don't want her here. Yet, I thought, that's a foolish thing to do, because all she'll say is, *she wasn't here*. She wasn't in person. Her body wasn't here." "After the voice, what came next?" "Well, it was shortly after that we started hearing these other voices." "Did you hear those voices?" "All of them, yes. All four." "Did they sound alike or did they sound different?" "The men had deep rough voices, but I could tell them apart. And the ladies were all subtle voices and I couldn't tell *them* apart, except when they told me." "Did you ever hear two voices at the same time?" "I don't believe so. However, Mrs. Snow and Mrs. Elliott were there at the same time. That is, *they said* they were. That was when Henry Anglin was giving us so much trouble and they had to carry him back to his grave." "Let's talk about anything that you have actually seen move." "I saw these notes that were folded. Sometimes as many as ten or fifteen notes a day." "From an enclosed room?" "Well, the doors weren't closed between the rooms, but I'd be sitting at the table eating something, and all of a sudden, I'd see one fall. I'd look up toward the ceiling and there'd be one up there." "Most of these notes were signed 'Mrs. Elliott'?" "Yes. Later she signed them. At first, Elie and then El. Now after my wife came back from Daingerfield she, too, would send me notes through Andy. I was working in my shop and Andy would bring me a note written with numbers, in code. 1 was A, 2 was B, and so forth. I hated to take the time to decipher those things, but I would sit down and find out what they said. In one note she asked me if I didn't 'lose' some weight." "Did your wife ever write you a note in longhand or in block letters?" "No." "Was there any similarity in the writing of your wife's notes and those notes that later came down from the ceiling?" "I can't say, but Mrs. Elliott had been after me to lose weight. I thought it was peculiar—that my wife came from Daingerfield and asked about my losing weight also." "Mrs. Elliott was a contemporary of your wife?" "She died in 1963. About a year before we moved here." "Were those two women very close in life?" "Not particularly. They were neighbors." "What about Mrs. Snow?" "She was peculiar." "What objects did you see move in person?" "I saw a heavy pair of shoes lift themselves off the floor and fly right over my bed and land on the opposite side of the bed." "Did they land fast or did they land slowly?" "It was just as if I'd picked them up and thrown them. Andy's house shoes came the same way. I've watched the cat being lifted up about a foot from where he was sitting and just be suspended for several seconds and it didn't fall on the floor. I saw a can of insect spray which was sitting on the cabinet come over and suspend itself right over that opening, and spray into that little room, and I was nearly suffocated. I had to open the doors or the insect spray would have got me." "You weren't holding the can?" "No." "I am particularly interested in anything where you were *actually* present when movement occurred, or voices were heard." "I've seen my clothes fly through the air as I was coming home." "Did these things occur whether your wife was physically in the house or not?" "Yes." "Did anything ever happen while neither your son nor your wife was at home but you were alone?" "I believe so." "Your wife had some personal shock in 1951, I believe. When her best friend died suddenly. Do you feel her mental state changed as a result?" "Very gradually, yes. She was very happy, though, when she found out she was going to have another child, because she thought this would make up for the loss of her friend. She was just crazy about him." "Now, when was the first time you noticed there was something wrong with her mentally?" "In 1960 my wife took over her daughter's room. She stopped up all the windows with newspapers scotch-taped against the wall and hung a blanket in each window of the bedroom." "Why did she do that?" "She felt someone was *spying on her*. At the office, she took the telephone apart, and adding machines and typewriters, looking for microphones to see who was spying on her." "But the phenomena themselves did not start until you moved into this house?" "That's right."

I thanked Mr. Beaird for his honest testimony, for he had not claimed anything beyond or different from his original report to me. I took the voluminous handwritten notes and the letters pertaining to the case and went back to New York to study them. This would take some time since I planned to compare the handwriting in the notes with samples of actual ordinary handwriting by both Mrs. Beaird and Andy. I didn't, for a moment, think that the notes had been written consciously by either one of them and simply thrown at Mr. Beaird in the ordinary way. Quite obviously Mr. Beaird was no fool, and any such clumsy attempt at fake phenomena would not have gone unnoticed, but there are other possibilities that could account for the presence of either Mrs. Beaird's or Andy's handwriting in the notes, if indeed there was that similarity.

There were already, clearly visible to me, certain parallels between this case and the Bell Witch case of Tennessee. Vengeance was being wrought on Howard Beaird by some entity or entities for alleged wrongs, in this case his failure to execute minor orders given him. But there were other elements differing greatly from the classic case. In the Bell Witch situation there was not present, in the household, anyone who could be classed as psychotic. In Tyler we have two individuals capable of supplying unused psychic energies. One definitely psychotic, the other on the borderline, or at least psychoneurotic.

I then decided to examine the notes written in this peculiar style longhand, almost always in block letters but upper case letters in the middle of words where they do not belong. It became immediately clear to me that this was a crude way of disguising the handwriting and was not used for any other reason. It is of course a fact that no one can effectively disguise his handwriting to fool the expert. He may think so, but an expert graphologist can always trace the peculiarities of a person's handwriting back to the original writer provided samples are available to compare the two handwritings letter by letter, word for word. Some of the notes were outright infantile. For instance, on December 6, 1965, a note read "My power is decreasing, I'm going back to Mack. I must hurry. I would like to come home but I don't guess I will. I love you. Please give me a Yule gift. I can't restore my power. I am allowed only three a year. Phone police." What the cryptic remark, "I am allowed only three a year," is supposed to mean is not explained.

Sometimes Howard Beaird played right into the hands of the unknown writer. The Sunday morning after he and Andy had spent the night at a motel because of the goings on in the house, he received the notice of a package at the post office. He knew that he couldn't get it except by noon on a week day, so he asked aloud, "Is this notice about anything important, as I don't want to come in from the hospital if it doesn't amount to anything?" A few seconds later a note fluttered down from the ceiling reading only "something." That of course was not a satisfactory answer such as an adult or reasonable person would give. It sounded more like a petulant child having a game. On December 6, 1965, a note materialized equally mysteriously, reading, "I don't want to admit to Mack that I'm nutty." Another note dated December 6, 1965, simply read, "Howard got jilted." Another note read "My powers were restored by the Houston witch. Call the police and ask about her." There doesn't seem to be any great difference between the notes signed by Henry Anglin or by Mrs. Elliott or not signed at all by someone intimating that they were the work of Mrs. Beaird. The letters and the formation of the words are similar. A note dated December 8, 1965, read, "Dear Howard, I love you. I have been wrong. I want to come home but I don't want stupid Mack to know I am unusual. I am really two people. If things end I won't remember nothin'. I can be in three places in one. I love you and Junior. Please dear."

The note signed "Dorothy Kilgallen," mentioned previously and received by Howard Beaird December 22, 1965, reads, "Dear Mr. Beaird: Mrs. Elliott told me about what all has happened to your family and what Henry Anglin is responsible for. It is very tragic. He is the reason I am dead because he changed my pills. Good night and good luck." Having been personally acquainted with the late Hearst columnist Dorothy Kilgallen, I am quite certain that she would not have expressed herself in this manner, dead or alive.

A note signed Pont Thornton dated December 23, 1965, reads, "Dear Howard P. S. an Andy: I no yu well. I no yu good. I don't drinck much do yu haf had hardships. Anglin is a mean man. I am smarter than Henry Lee. I am a distant kin of Abe Lincoln and Lewis Armstrong and Sam Davis Junior and Jon F. Kenede." Not only was the note atrociously misspelled but it listed several quite improbable relationships. When writing as Mrs. Elliott the personality is much more concise and logical than when the writer is supposed to be Henry Anglin or Mrs. Beaird. But despite the difference in style the letters are very similar. Of course since the notes came down for almost three years it is to be expected that there are some differences in both style and appearance between them.

On September 17, 1967, Howard Beaird observed, "About

9 or 10 p.m. Andy heard Mrs. Elliott call. She told him he could talk to her and that mother could not hear so he did and apparently mother knew nothing of it. Just as I was getting ready for bed I heard Mrs. Elliott calling me. *The sound seemed to come toward the kitchen and as Andy and Johnny were watching TV in her bedroom I went to the kitchen.* Mrs. Elliott called me several more times and the sound then seemed to be coming from my room. She said that Johnny couldn't hear me so I tried to talk to her but Andy said she told him she never could hear me. Anyway before going to bed I found a very small piece of paper folded so small on the floor in the hall and also a South Side Bank deposit slip folded near it. The small note said 'Be very generous. Say hi to me. Mrs. Snow.' The larger note said, 'Don't be stingy Sam be a generous Joe. George Swiney.' After I had gone to bed I heard Mrs. Elliott calling me several times but could never make her hear me answer. Just as I was about to go to sleep, Andy came in and said Mrs. Elliott told him she had left me a note on the floor. Just as I got up to look for it a note dropped in the chair next to my bed. *I took it to the kitchen to get my glasses and it said, 'Howard, I hope there won't be any slugs. Try to be generous, you have a lot of money. There's so much you could get you, John and Andy.'* This was followed by a list of objects, clothing primarily, which he could get for his family on her suggestion. Howard Beaird tried to talk to Mrs. Elliott to ask her where all that alleged money was but he could never get an answer to that.

On September 29, 1967, Howard Beaird noticed that Mrs. Elliott came to visit him around 7:30 p.m. He can't understand how she can make him hear her when she calls him by name and then make it impossible for him to hear the rest of her. Apparently the rest of the conversation has to be relayed through Andy. On the other hand, if he speaks loudly enough she can hear him. That night Mrs. Elliott informed him that a Mr. Quinn had been by earlier. A little later Mr. Quinn himself came back and Howard Beaird actually heard him call, but he could hear nothing else, and again Andy had to be the interpreter. Andy said that Mr. Quinn sounded like a robot talking, and that, of course, made sense to Mr. Beaird, since he knew that Quinn, who had lost his voice due to cancer prior to his death, used an instrument held to his throat to enable him to talk. The late Mr. Quinn apparently wanted to know how some of the people back in Grand Saline were, including a Mrs. Drake, Mr. and Mrs. Watkins, and the McMullens. This information, of course, could not have been known to Andy, who had been much too young at the time the Beairds knew these people in the town where they formerly lived.

Mrs. Elliott also explained the reason she and the other spirits were able to be with Mr. Beaird that evening was that they had been given time off for the holidays—because of Halloween, although that was a little early for All Hallow's Eve. Mr. Beaird thought it peculiar that spirits get furloughs from whatever place they are in.

On September 30, 1967, Beaird had heard nothing at all from Mrs. Elliott during the day. Andy had been out pretty late that night and Mr. Beaird was asleep when he came in. Sometime after, Andy woke him and said that Mrs. Elliott had left him a note. They found it on his bed. It read, "Howard, think about what I said. Are you going to do it Monday. Elliott."Just below it was a note reading, "John wants a vacuum cleaner and a purse. Junior wants a coat for school and some banjo strings. Hiram." Now the remarkable thing about this note is that the first part was definitely in the handwriting of Mrs. Beaird, while the second part was a crude note put together with a lot of capital letters where they did not belong and generally disorganized. Hiram Quinn, the alleged writer, was of course a very sick man for some time prior to his passing. When Howard Beaird confronted the alleged Mrs. Elliott with the fact that her note was written in the handwriting of his wife, she shrugged it off by explaining that she could write like anybody she wished.

On October 2, 1967, Mr. Beaird noted, "About 7:30 p.m. Mrs. Snow called my name. I was in the kitchen and the voice seemed to come from the back part of the house where Andy and John were. The voice sounded exactly like Mrs. Elliott's and although I could hear it plainly enough and answered aloud immediately I could hear nothing else and Andy had to tell me what she said. She just wanted to tell me about my stamp business and how John had been. She barely could hear me and told Andy to turn off the attic fan and for me to go into my room and close the door so she could hear. She couldn't explain how I could hear her call my name and then hear nothing more and said it was some kind of 'law.' "

The notes signed by Mrs. Elliott from that period onward frequently looked as if they had been written by Mrs. Beaird. The handwriting is unquestionably hers. That is to say it looks like hers. Howard Beaird does not doubt that the notes were genuinely materialized in a psychic sense. On October 23 he had dozed off to sleep several times and on one occasion was awakened by the rustling of papers on the floor beside his bed. He was alone in the room at the time. He turned the light on and found a sort of pornographic magazine folded up on the floor. Andy came in at that point and explained that Mrs. Elliott had told him she had found this magazine in Mrs. Beaird's room. She said that Mrs. Beaird had gotten it at the beauty shop and the piece of paper was torn from it. On the note was printed "Somebody loves you," signed underneath, El.

On November 12, 1967, a Sunday, Howard Beaird heard Mrs. Elliott talk to him. She advised him that he should go to Mrs. Beaird's room and look for some nudist pictures and also some hand-drawn pictures of naked men and women. Mr. Beaird found all these things but his wife denied any knowledge of them. The following night, November 13, 1967, was particularly remarkable in the kind of phenomena experienced by Howard Beaird. "Mrs. Elliott came by before I left for the shop and told me to look for some more lewd pictures. I found some and destroyed them. Mrs. Elliott told me to be sure and tear them up in front of John and maybe she would quit drawing them, and also quit buying the nudist magazine pictures. Later that night, about 9:15, Mrs. Elliott called me on the telephone. *That's the first time I ever talked to a ghost on the telephone.* I could understand what she said on the phone, yet I could never hear anything except her calling my name when I was at home. Of course all she said on the phone was to come home. I then talked to Andy and he said she wanted me to come home right then and get some more drawings and nudist magazines from John's hiding places. I did go home and got the pictures and went back to the shop after I had destroyed them."

Some of the notes showed the underlying conflict, imagined or real, between the young boy and his father which was of much concern to "guardian angel" Mrs. Elliott. On January 11, 1968, a note read, "Howard, I need to write you notes. Junior has had to worry so much. Why do you mind him coming with me? He would be happy. It would be right for him not to worry. I agree he must get an education but at seventeen he could get a course and then to college. In the meantime I will help John and him. He could play music and he would be great at seventeen. He would also like to take care of the house. John would get so much better. You would be better financially and Junior could get better. This is the only thing I will allow or I will take him with me if he wants to . . . He said he would tell me to go and wouldn't go but that wouldn't change him from wanting to. You had better pay attention cause he wants to come. I have all the divine right to take him. El." This threat by the spirit of Mrs. Elliott to take the young boy with her into the spirit world did not sit lightly with his father, of course. Analyzed on its face value, it has the ring of a petulant threat a retarded youngster would make against his parents if he didn't get his way. If Mrs. Elliott was the spirit of a mature and rational person then this kind of threat didn't seem, to me, to be in character with the personality of the alleged Mrs. Elliott.

The following night, January 12, 1968, the communicator wrote, "Howard, I have the divine right. I will prove it by taking Junior and I take him tonight. You don't love him at all. You don't care about anyone." Mrs. Elliott had not taken Andy by January 15, but she let Howard know that she might do so anyway any time now. In fact, her notes sounded more and more like a spokesman for Andy if he wanted to complain about life at home but didn't have the courage to say so consciously and openly. On January 18, Mrs. Elliott decided she wasn't going to take the boy after all. She had promised several times before that she would not come back any longer and that her appearance was the last one. But she always broke this pledge.

By now any orthodox psychologist or even parapsychologist would assume that the young man was materially involved not only in the composition of the notes but in actually writing them. I don't like to jump to conclusions needlessly, especially not when a prejudice concerning the method of communication would clearly be involved in assuming that the young man did the actual writing. But

I decided to continue examining each and every word and to see whether the letters or the words themselves gave me any clue as to what human hand had actually written them, if any. It appeared clear to me by now that some if not all of the notes purporting to be the work of Mrs. Elliott were in the hand of Mrs. Beaird. But it was not a very good copy of her handwriting. Rather did it seem to me that someone had attempted to write in Mrs. Beaird's hand who wasn't actually Mrs. Beaird. As for the other notes, those signed by Henry Anglin, Hiram Quinn and those unsigned but seemingly the work of Mrs. Beaird herself, they had certain common denominators amongst them. I had asked Mr. Beaird to supply me with adequate examples of the handwriting of both Andy and Mrs. Beaird. That is to say handwritten notes not connected in any way with the psychic phenomena at the house. I then studied these examples and compared them with the notes which allegedly came from nowhere or which materialized by falling from the ceiling in front of a very astonished Mr. Beaird.

I singled out the following letters as being characteristic of the writer, whoever he or she may be. The capital letter T, the lower case e, lower case p, g, y, r, and capital B, C, L, and the figure 9. All of these appeared in a number of notes. They also appear in the sample of Andy's handwriting, in this case a list of song titles which he liked and which he was apparently going to learn on his guitar. There is no doubt in my mind that the letters in the psychic notes and the letters on Andy's song list are identical. *That is to say that they were written by the same hand.* By that I do not mean to say, necessarily, that Andy wrote the notes. I do say, however, that the hand used to create the psychic notes is the same hand used consciously by Andy Beaird when writing notes of his own. I am less sure, but suspect, that even the notes seemingly in the handwriting of his mother are also done in the same fashion and also traceable to Andy Beaird.

On December 7, 1965, one of the few drawings in the stack of notes appeared. It showed a man in a barber chair and read, among other annotations, "Aren't the barbers sweet, ha ha." It should be remembered that Andy's great ambition in life was to become a barber. In fact, when I met and interviewed him he was going to barber school.

What then is the meaning of all this? Let us not jump to conclusions and say Andy Beaird wrote the notes somehow unobserved, smuggled them into Mr. Beaird's room somehow unnoticed, and made them fall from the ceiling seemingly by their own volition, somehow without Mr. Beaird noticing this. In a number of reported instances this is a possibility, but in the majority of cases it simply couldn't have happened in this manner, not unless Howard Beaird was not a rational individual and was, in fact, telling me lies. I have no doubt that Mr. Beaird is telling me the truth and that he is a keen and rational observer. Consequently the burden of truth for the validity of the phenomena does not rest on his gift of observation, but on the possibility of producing such paranormal occurrences despite their seeming improbability yet reconciling this with the ominous fact that they show strong indications of being Andy Beaird's handwriting.

We must recognize the tension existing for many years in the Beaird household, the unhappy condition in which young Andy found himself as he grew up, and the fact that for a number of years he was an introspected and suppressed human being unable to relate properly to the outside world and forced to find stimulation where he could. Under such conditions certain forces within a young person can be exteriorized and become almost independent of the person himself. Since these forces are part of the unconscious in the person and therefore not subject to the logical controls of the conscious mind, they are, in fact, childish and frequently irrational. They are easily angered and easily appeased and, in general, behave in an infantile fashion. By the same token these split-off parts of personality are capable of performing physical feats, moving objects, materializing things out of nowhere and, in general, contravening the ordinary laws of science. This we know already because cases of poltergeists have occurred with reasonable frequency in many parts of the world. In the case of the Beaird family, however, we have two other circumstances which must be taken into account. The first is the presence in the house of not one but two emotionally unstable individuals. Mrs. Beaird's increasing divorce from reality, leading to a state of schizophrenia, must have freed some powerful forces within her. Her seemingly unconscious preoccupation with some aspects of sex indicates a degree of frustration on her part yet an inability to do anything about it at the conscious level. We have long recognized that the power supply used to perform psychic phenomena is the same power inherent in the life force or the sexual drive in man, and when this force is not used in the ordinary way it can be diverted to the supernormal expression, which in this case took the form of poltergeist phenomena. We have, therefore, in the Beaird case, a tremendous reservoir of untapped psychic energy subject to very little conscious control on the part of the two individuals in whose bodies these energies were stored and developed.

Were the entities purporting to use these facilities to express themselves beyond the grave actually the people who had once lived and died in the community? Were they, in fact, who they claimed to be, or were they simply being re-enacted unconsciously perhaps by the split-off part of the personalities of both Andy and Mrs. Beaird? Since Howard Beaird has examined the signature of one of those entities, at least, and found it to be closely similar, if not identical, with the signature of the person while alive, and since, in that particular case, access to the signature was not possible to either Andy or Mrs. Beaird, I'm inclined to believe that actual non-physical entities were, in fact, using the untapped energies of these two unfortunate individuals to express themselves in the physical world. Additional evidence, I think, would be the fact that in several cases the names and certain details concerning the personalities of several individuals whom Howard Beaird knew in their former residence in Grand Saline were not known or accessible to either his wife or the young man. I am not fully satisfied that there could not have been some form of collusion between Andy and these so-called spirit entities in creating the phenomena, but if there was such collusion it was on the unconscious level. It is my view that Andy's unexpressed frustrations and desires were picked up by some of these discarnate entities and mingled with their own desire to continue involving themselves in earth conditions and thus became the driving force in making the manifestations possible.

What about the fact that Andy Beaird's handwriting appears in the majority of the notes? If Andy did not write these notes physically himself, could they have been produced in some other manner? There is no doubt in my mind that in at least a large percentage of the notes Andy could not have written them physically and dropped them in front of his father without Mr. Beaird noticing it. Yet, these very same notes also bear unmistakable signs that they are the work of Andy Beaird's hand. Therefore the only plausible solution is to assume that a spiritual part of Andy's body was used to create the notes in the same way in which seemingly solid objects have, at times, been materialized and dematerialized. This is known as a "physical" phenomenon and it is not entirely restricted to poltergeist cases but has, on occasion, been observed with solid objects which were moved from one place to another, or which appeared at a place seemingly out of nowhere, or disappeared from a place without leaving any trace. The phenomenon is not unique nor particularly new. What is unique, or nearly so in the case of the Beaird family of Tyler, Texas, is the fact that here the obvious is not the most likely explanation. I do not think Andy Beaird wrote those notes consciously. I do believe that his writing ability was used by the entities expressing themselves through him. I believe that Andy was telling the truth when he said he was surprised by the appearance of the notes and at no time did he have knowledge of their contents except when one of the other spirit entities informed him about them. The same applies, of course, to Mrs. Beaird. In the phenomena known as automatic writing, the hand of a living person, normally a fully rational and conscious individual, is used to express the views, memories and frequently the style of writing of a dead individual. The notes which fluttered down from the ceiling at the Beaird home are not of the same kind. Here the paper had first to be taken from one place and impressed with pencil writing in the hand of another person before the note itself could be materialized in plain view of witnesses. This is far more complex than merely impressing the muscular apparatus of a human being to write certain words in a certain way.

Why then did the phenomena cease when the Beairds moved from one home to another if the entities expressing themselves through Andy and Mrs. Beaird had not found satisfaction? There was no need for them to simply leave off just because the Beairds moved from one house to the other. There must have been something in the atmosphere of the first house that in combination with the untapped psychic energies of Andy and Mrs. Beaird provided a fertile ground for the phenomena.

Apparently some disturbances have continued in the former Beaird home, while none have been reported by them in their new house. The current owners of the old Beaird home, however, refused to discuss such matters as psychic phenomena in the house. They are fully convinced that their fundamentalist religion will allow them to take care of these occurrences. To them psychic phenomena *are all the work of the devil.*

And so the devil in Tyler, Texas, may yet erupt once again to engulf a family, if not an entire community, with the strange and frightening goings on which, for three years, have plagued the Beaird family to the point of emotional and physical exhaustion. The Beairds themselves are out of danger. Andy has grown up and his untapped powers will unquestionably be used in more constructive channels as the years go by. Mrs. Beaird has assumed her rightful position in her husband's house and has closed the door on her unhappy past. Howard Beaird, the main victim of all the terrible goings on between 1965 and 1968, is satisfied that they are nothing now but memories. He has no desire to bring them back. His sole interest in my publishing an account of these incredible happenings was to inform the public and to help those who might have similar experiences.

VIRGINIA

With one exception no state in the Union is more often connected with hauntings, in the public mind, than is Virginia. That is so because the rolling hills south of Washington, dotted as they are with magnificent manor houses, many of them dating back to colonial days, seem to be the kind of atmosphere ghosts prefer. The sole exception to this public image are the New England mansions perched perilously atop storm-swept cliffs where, usually during storms, the ghosts of sea captains still walk and the unwary traveler is frightened to death. That, at least, is the impression still rampant among the uninstructed, although it is perfectly true that there are sea captains in New England manor houses walking long after their time on earth has expired.

But Virginia, which is primarily horse country and was settled originally by people from the Anglo-Saxon countries, is very much like England in many respects. Even the ghosts, such as they are, that continue a shadowy existence in some of the estates and plantation houses are similar in their habits to those found in English stately homes. Almost "the first state in the Union" because of its early connection with the creation of the country and because it was the home of so many of the leaders of the Revolutionary War, Virginia must be considered the closest to an oligarchic state in America. Divided among a small number of illustrious families, Virginia has for a long time been a feudal barony of sorts, and to this very day the great houses attest to the way this first among the thirteen colonies developed. Even though the plantations that were once the life blood of these houses are no longer in existence, the houses themselves continue to flourish because the Virginians have a keen sense of history and tradition. Many of the houses, of course, have been restored because of decay. Nevertheless, there are still some which have stood the test of time and survived from their seventeenth- or eighteenth-century origins almost intact to this day.

Foremost among such manor houses is the magnificent estate of Westover on the James River. Built originally in 1730 by William Byrd II, the man who founded Richmond, it stands amid an 11,000-acre working farm. The formal gardens surrounding the house are open to the public, but the house itself is not. A magnificent eighteenth-century ceiling in the entrance hall matches the paneling of the walls. Throughout the manor house there is evidence of grandeur. This is not the home of a country squire but of a statesman of great wealth. When William Byrd was killed during the Revolutionary War the widow sold the original furniture in 1813. Eventually the house passed into the hands of Mrs. Bruce Crane Fisher. Her grandfather had bought the house in 1921 and became the eleventh owner since the plantation had been in existence. Mrs. Fisher has furnished the house in recent years with authentic eighteenth-century English and European furniture to restore it as closely as possible to the original appearance. The Georgian house stands amid tall old trees and consists of a central portion and two wings. The central portion has three stories of elegant brickwork and two tall chimneys. The two wings were originally not connected to the center portion of the house, but the right wing had to be restored in 1900 since it had been damaged by fire from a shelling during the Civil War. At that time the two wings were also connected to the house and are now accessible directly from the main portion. The main entrance faces the James River and has the original wrought-iron entrance gate with stone eagles surmounting the gateposts. Thus, with minimal additions and restorations, the house today presents pretty much the same picture it did when it was first built in 1730.

Colonel Byrd took his beautiful daughter Evelyn, pronounced *Eevelyn* in Virginia, to London for the coronation of King George I. That was in 1717 when the great men of the colonies, when they could afford it, would come to the mother country when the occasion arose. Evelyn, at the time, was eighteen years old and her father decided to leave her in England to be educated. Soon he received disquieting news from his confidants at the London court. It appeared that Evelyn had been seen with a certain Charles Mordaunt and that the two young people were hopelessly in love with each other. Normally this would be a matter for rejoicing, but not so in this case. Charles was an ardent Roman Catholic and the grandson of the Earl of Peterborough. Colonel Byrd, on the other hand, was politically and personally a staunch Protestant, and the idea of his daughter marrying into the enemy camp, so to speak, was totally unacceptable to him. Immediately he ordered her to return to Westover and Evelyn had no choice but to obey. As soon as she arrived at the family plantation she went into isolation. She refused to see any other suitors her father sent her or to consider, or even to discuss, the possibility of marriage.

This went on for some time, and Evelyn quite literally "pined away" to death. Some weeks before her death, however, she had a very emotional discussion with her best friend, Anne Harrison. The two girls were walking up a hill when Evelyn, feeling faint, knew that her days were numbered. She turned to her friend and promised her that she would return after her death. Mrs. Harrison did not take this very seriously, but she knew that Evelyn was not well and her death did not come as a shock. The following spring, after Westover had somehow returned to a degree of normalcy and the tragic events of the previous year were not so strongly in evidence, Mrs. Harrison was walking in the garden sadly remembering what had transpired the year before. Suddenly she saw her old friend standing beside her in a dazzling white gown. The vision then drifted forward two steps, waved its hand at her and smiled. An instant later it had vanished. At the time of her untimely death Evelyn Byrd had been twenty-nine years of age, but in the apparition she seemed much younger and lovelier than she had appeared toward the end of her life. The specter has reappeared from time to time to a number of people, both those who live in the area and those who are guests at Westover. A lady who lives nearby who has been there for nearly three decades saw her in the mid 1960s. She had been coming out of the front door one summer and was walking down the path when she looked back toward the house and saw a woman come out behind her. At first she thought it was a friend and stopped at the gate to wait for her. When the woman came closer, however, she didn't recognize her. There was something very strange about the woman coming toward her. There seemed to be a glow all about her person, her black hair, and the white dress. When the woman had arrived close to her she stopped and seemed to sink into the ground.

On December 11, 1929, some guests from Washington were staying at Westover, and on the evening of their arrival the conversation turned to ghosts. The house was then owned by Mr. and Mrs. Richard H. Crane, who explained that they themselves had not seen the ghost during their tenancy. One of the house guests retired to the room assigned to her on the side of the house overlooking the great gates from which one has a fine view into the formal gardens. Sometime that night Mrs. Crane awoke and went to the window. There was no apparent reason for her behavior. It was quite dark outside and very quiet. As she glanced out the window she saw the figure of Evelyn Byrd. She described the apparition to her hosts as filmy, nebulous and cloudy, so transparent no features could be distinguished, only a gauzy texture of a woman's form. The figure seemed to be floating a little above the lawn and almost on the level of the window itself. As she looked at it almost transfixed, the apparition acknowledged her by raising her hand and motioning to her to go back into the room and away from the window. The gesture seemed so imperative that the house guest obeyed it.

When I requested permission to investigate the house I was politely denied access. Perhaps the present owners are afraid that I might induce the lovely Evelyn to leave Westover for a better life in paradise, and that would never do, for Westover is, after all, the nearest thing to paradise on earth, at least to an eighteenth-century lass whose lover has gone away. Had I had the opportunity to come into contact with her through some reputable medium perhaps

I might have reunited the two in a land and under conditions where her stern father Colonel Byrd could no longer keep them apart.

Another famous Virginia mansion is Blandfield, which has more than one ghost. In the late 1960s the Richmond *Times Dispatch* made a survey of some of the better ghost houses in the area. Tom Howard interviewed a number of people who owned such houses and he also journeyed up to Blandfield to interview the owner. Here is his report. "Blandfield, an eighteenth century mansion in Essex County, has been frequented by a variety of spooks for two centuries. They've come as eerie lights in the night and wispy figures of men and women stalking through the halls.

"Mrs. William Nash Beverley, wife of the owner, related that about five years ago house guests reported apparitions on two occasions. The first was in a long, flowered dress walking across the upstairs hall. Everyone searched the home, but the stranger wasn't found. Two days later, a second guest saw a woman, in a long, dark skirt, cross a downstairs hall, and enter a room. Again an investigation found no one, said Mrs. Beverley.

"The most recent episode came several months before, she said. Mrs. Beverley recounted the experience. She and two dogs were in the downstairs library one afternoon and the only other person in the house was an ill relative who she knew was asleep in an upstairs bedroom. Suddenly, heavy footsteps sounded in the room directly overhead. Startled, she listened. The dogs sprang to their feet, hair bristling.

"First I thought I would take a shotgun and go up, said Mrs. Beverley. Then I thought how silly that was. But I was uneasy, so I put a leash on each dog and we rushed up the steps. As I went up the steps, the dogs became more excited, their hair stood straight up.

"She went straight to the bedroom of her relative, who was lying quietly in bed, still asleep. The dogs strained at the leash and pulled toward the room where she heard the heavy footsteps. She opened the door and the dogs bounded in fiercely . . . but there was no one there. She explored every hiding place in the room, but found no trace of a living human being. The dogs quieted down and she decided that, at last, she had heard one of the famed Blandfield ghosts."

There is a rocking chair ghost at Shirley plantation in Chase City and another rocking chair ghost at Ash Lawn, once the home of President James Monroe, and the ghost of Governor Kemper is said to still inhabit Walnut Hill, his erstwhile home. I have reported a number of such cases in an earlier book called *Ghosts I've Met*. In fact, the area around Charlottesville, which I investigated personally in 1965, abounds with authentic hauntings.

It is just possible that someone who is psychic and who might have passed the building now housing the Health, Education and Welfare Department in Charlottesville might feel peculiar, perhaps a chill or two, perhaps only a sense of displacement in time. On that spot there was once a magnificent house built around 1820 in the style of the Roman country houses of Andrea Palladino. James Dinsmore, an architect brought there by Thomas Jefferson, designed the house for Francis B. Dyer, a lawyer. Later it passed into the hands of William B. Fitch, but eventually the house changed hands again and just before the Civil War it belonged to a certain Eugene Davis, a man prominently connected with Episcopal Sunday school work. He was the oldest son of Professor John A. G. Davis, Chairman of the University of Charlottesville. The professor was killed during one of the student riots of those days. Shortly afterwards, when another son, James Maury Morris Davis, occupied the cottage in the yard, the first uncanny experiences took place. Studying late one night, young Davis heard the gate click and footsteps sound along the hall. He opened the door but saw no one out there. This repeated itself numerous times. When the house passed into the hands of Major Horace Jones, who headed a boys' preparatory school in Charlottesville, the phenomena continued. Some of the students who had been assigned the cottage to live in complained of footsteps in the yard. The gate would click open and shut and there never was anyone there. It was assumed that the murdered professor was checking up on his former home. The phenomena continued until after Major Jones died in 1904. When the cottage was eventually pulled down and replaced by the present structure, the noises stopped, but there is no telling what a psychic person might feel standing on the spot where the hauntings used to be.

There is a quietly elegant old frame house at 6321 Monument Avenue in Richmond which belies its violent history. The Richmond *News Leader* of April 7, 1967, told its story for the first time to a broader public. The owner at the time, Donald B. Wiltshire, had seen the ghost of a little old man with a chin beard as he was going to bed. He was so surprised by the apparition that he fell on the top step. Mr. Wiltshire employed the services of a historian, Mrs. Roger Mann, to dig into the past of his house. Mrs. Mann discovered that nineteen bodies had originally been buried in two graveyards somewhere on the Wiltshire property. Moreover, there was good reason to assume that half a million dollars was buried somewhere on the premises. To date that treasure has not been recovered but it has a basis in fact. In 1821 the house on Monument Avenue belonged to a certain Dan Green who worked in a bank. At the time Mr. Green was accused of absconding with $500,000. Since the money was never found the teller was acquitted. The only things remotely relating to the treasure were some coins found by men excavating for a swimming pool a few years ago, but they didn't add up to $500,000.

Andy Wilkins is a young ghost fancier of southwest Virginia. He has kept me informed of some of the goings on in the area, notably of Berry Hill, a magnificent manor house not far from Westover. In fact, it is built on land once part of the Westover estate. Built and owned by the Bruce family, which is related by marriage to the owners of Westover, the estate is now empty. A few years ago a certain Fred Watkins bought Berry Hill as a wedding gift for his son, but when the young people tried to spend the night in it they were frightened out of it by footsteps and the uncanny presence of something they could not see. Since then the house has been closed. The building is being kept up like a museum, but there is only a caretaker on the grounds. Allegedly the ghost is the son of the original builder, who died childless but resents that the house passed out of the hands of the Bruce family to strangers.

White Marsh in Gloucester County is a magnificent plantation house now owned by Mr. and Mrs. William Ingles and a private residence. In 1654, 3200 acres of land were granted to a certain Lewis Burwell whose descendant the present owner is. Today only 2000 acres remain. The house has passed through several hands since the Burwells owned it. The present White Marsh was built in 1798 and enlarged by the Tabb family in 1883. There is a legend that a curse was put on the place at the time when John Tabb bought it, a curse that was to last until the property was returned to its "rightful owners," presumably the sons of Thomas Rootes, who had sold the place to the Tabbs. But apparently the curse was not very effective, for the Tabb family lived at White Marsh undisturbed until 1906, when the place passed into the hands of Willie Buries, who made extensive changes, replacing the Georgian style with Greek revival. When the house passed into the hands of the current owners, the Ingles, they had to re-do the house to bring it back to its original appearance. Constance Ingles moved into the house in 1948. She made extensive inquiries about anything dramatic that might have transpired in the house in its long history. She discovered no murders or suicides, but apparently several infant children of the Tabb family had died there. There was an account of a ghostly apparition, however, according to which mother Tabb was seen entering a certain room, opening a bureau drawer, removing all the child's clothes, shaking them out and folding them and returning them to the drawer. Mrs. Ingles just knew that this concerned the room where their two oldest sons were living at the time and she always knew that it was young Bill's chest of drawers the ghostly mother Tabb was opening. A neighbor had actually seen mother Tabb passing her on the stairs with her swishing taffeta skirts.

Constance Ingles has a long history of ESP and experiences that can only be classed as memories from a previous lifetime. She had seen her first ghost at the age of sixteen when she was a student at Bennington College West. This was at a small inn near Seneca, New York. At White Marsh Mrs. Ingles has not actually seen any ghosts, but she has shared, with her husband and their little daughter, an auditory experience that has left them very much impressed with the fact that there are unseen presences at their home. Three or four weeks after they had moved into the house Mrs. Ingles was awakened by the sound of heavy footsteps in the attic proceeding from the north side of the house to the center. Reluctant to wake up her husband, Mrs. Ingles wondered who was walking about when she heard her little daughter, then four years old, call

"Mommy, who is that walking in the attic?" Now sure that she was not hallucinating, she awakened her husband. Together they decided to investigate. The footsteps were directly over their heads then. A moment later they halted again, and then something seemed to land on the roof of the one-story wing, right under their bedroom window. They dashed to the window and heard a loud thud as something seemed to hit the ground. Seconds after that there was heard the sound of horses' hoofs going up the lane. The next morning they investigated and found hoofprints under the window. They checked whether one of their horses had escaped from the barn, but none had. Also, the round window in the attic, on the south side where the footsteps had halted, cannot be opened. Mr. Ingles, who is a firm disbeliever in such matters as psychic phenomena, was impressed.

Although she has not seen this herself, Mrs. Ingles, all the children, and some of their friends have frequently reported the appearance of something filmy-white in the gardens. Marguerite Dupont Lee has reported some of the traditional legends associated with White Marsh in her books. One of them concerns the sound of a party, music, and dancing going on in the house when there is no one there. Another one deals with a woman rocking in a chair in the northeast bedroom, the room once occupied by General Lee during his visit to White Marsh. A year after the Ingleses had moved into White Marsh they employed a black couple from Philadelphia named Henry and Frances Parker. Mrs. Ingles is quite sure the couple were not aware of these traditions when they first came to the house. Shortly after their arrival the butler came to Mrs. Ingles on a Sunday morning wondering if they had come home unexpectedly the afternoon before. They had not and she so informed the butler. He then reported that

Saturday afternoon, when the children had been sleeping and he and his wife had been in their room, they had heard someone playing the piano. Assuming that Mrs. Ingles had returned home and was playing the piano, he decided to leave the matter alone, but his wife insisted that it didn't sound like Mrs. Ingles playing. So he decided to go out and look. When he reached the stair landing, within perhaps two or three steps of the piano, the music stopped and there was a whooshing sound that moved toward the door to the back hall. Still shaken by this episode, the butler was even more impressed with the presence of something unseen. A few weeks later when he took Mrs. Ingles her morning coffee he explained that he and his wife had not slept all night because something was rocking in their room. When Mrs. Ingles pointed out that there was no rocking chair in that room, he explained that he knew that very well, but that their straight chair seemed to rock as if it had rockers under it.

Despite Mrs. Ingles's ESP leanings, things have been on the quiet side these past few years. It is conceivable that the ghosts of White Marsh have taken the Ingleses to their heart and do not wish to interfere with their lives by appearing before them. Ghosts have a way of staying dormant for long times, being unaware of the passage of time and content to relive their own most important moments.